TIME INNOVATIONS AND THE DEPLOYMENT OF MANPOWER

Time Innovations and the Deployment of Manpower

Attitudes and Options

PAUL RATHKEY
Head of Research
Jim Conway Foundation

Avebury

Aldershot · Brookfield USA · Hong Kong · Singapore · Sydney

© Jim Conway Foundation 1990

All rights reserved. No part of this publication may be reproduced, stored in a retrieval system, or transmitted in any form or by any means, electronic, mechanical, photocopying, recording or otherwise without the prior permission of Gower Publishing Company Limited.

Published by
Avebury
Gower Publishing Company Limited
Gower House
Croft Road
Aldershot
Hants GU11 3HR
England

Gower Publishing Company
Old Post Road
Brookfield
Vermont 05036
USA

British Library Cataloguing in Publication Data
Rathkey, Paul 1950-
  Time innovations and the deployment of manpower :
  attitudes and options
  1. Personnel. Time. Allocation
  I. Title
  331.257

  ISBN 0-566-07121-5

Printed in Great Britain by
Athenaeum Press Ltd, Newcastle upon Tyne.

Contents

	Foreword	vii
1.	**Aims and Objectives**	1
	Introduction	1
	Project focus	2
	Study areas and design	3
	Reducing working time: some assumptions and premises	4
2.	**Key Factors in Working Time Reductions**	6
	Introduction	6
	Productivity	7
	Occupational changes	9
	Industrial relations	13
	Labour market: the 'flexible firm'	16
	Working time trends and developments	23
	Summary	25
3.	**Trade Unions, Collective Bargaining, Flexibility and Reduced Working Time**	28
	Introduction	28
	The TUC and shorter working time	29
	Bargaining working time	30
	New working patterns	32
	Temporary work	34
	The 'flexible firm' debate and trade unions	35
	Working time developments: what price change?	36
	Trends in reduced working time	38
	Conclusions	39

4. Case studies of Work Re-organization and Time Innovations   45

    Introduction   45
    Methodology   46
    Case study 1: Five-crew shiftworking - A chemical company   47
    Case study 2: Part-time working - A textile company   47
    Case study 3: Harmonization - A pharmaceutical company   48
    Case study 4: Flexible rostering - A study on the railways   49
    Conclusions from case studies   50

5. Working Time Preferences   57

    Introduction   57
    Choosing time contracts   58
    Desire for reduced hours   60
    Time Use   66
    Extra working hours   68
    Which route to shorter hours?   68

6. Varying Hours - Part time Work, Job Sharing and Overtime   73

    A   Part time work   73
    B   Job sharing   84
    C   Overtime   89

7. Working Week or Working Life?   98

    Working week preferences   98
    Shorter hours, employment and productivity   102
    Options and developments   102
    Legislation   103
    Holidays   104
    Sabbaticals   105

8. Developing Approaches to Annual Hours   107

    A   Flexi-time   107
    B   Shiftwork innovations   109
    C   Annual hours contracts/annual time commitments   113

9. Conclusions   116

    Working time options   117
    Voluntary vs negotiated hours reductions   118
    Future trends and directions - some possibilities   119

    Select Bibliography   122

    Appendix I   - Survey Questionnaire   123

    Appendix II - Survey Classification   132

Foreword

This study on time management, preferences and policy development is the thirteenth major project completed by the Foundation's Research Department. As on each previous occasion, in keeping with the policy of the Foundation's Trustees, it has been my responsibility to seek to publish the findings of the work. I would like to express our gratitude to the Gower Publishing Company Limited for undertaking this publication.

The Leverhulme Trust, who entirely funded the research, are especially thanked for their faith in our endeavours and I hope that they are satisfied with the final result.

I must make reference to Paul Rathkey who, as the Foundation's Head of Research, was responsible for the study and was the sole author of the final report. I would like to record my personal gratitude to the Foundation's administrative staff for the preparation of the report and, in particular, Alison Wharton and Sue Drinkhall for the unenviable task of ensuring that the entire script was camera ready for publication.

Andy Wood
Director
The Jim Conway Foundation
8 Yarm Road
Stockton on Tees
Cleveland
TS18 3NA

0642-613541/2

1 Aims and objectives

Introduction

Seventy years ago Bertrand Russell wrote:

> I think we may assume that, with the help of science...the whole community could be kept in comfort by means of four hours work a day. The dread of unemployment and loss of livelihood will no longer haunt men like a nightmare. (1)

Russell's assumption that advances in science and technology would lead to major improvements in living standards has largely been borne out. The view that such developments would radically reduce individual working time and consequently unemployment, however, has not. There has been a correlation between rising productivity and shorter working hours but advances in the former have greatly outstripped reductions in the latter. Machinery has replaced manual work — from agriculture, construction, manufacturing and even into the service industries — but notions of 'a day's work' or 'a week's work' have been little affected. Work is the guarantor of income and, regardless of its outcomes, the important thing is to be seen to be doing it during the hours allotted. This conservative approach to working time is coming under pressure — partly as a consequence of economic recession and technological developments but also as a result of sociological factors such as a decreasing birth rate, increased female participation rates, the development of equal opportunities and an ageing population. There is greater demand to enter the labour market and greater support is required for those failing to gain entry and those who have been ejected from it (the unemployed); as well as for those who have voluntarily left (many through early retirement) but who are continuing to live longer.

As a consequence working patterns are beginning to alter – part time work has increased, the 'informal economy' has grown and more flexible patterns of work are being developed (many to meet the demands of the family as an economic unit).

As living standards become increasingly dependent upon the distribution of work rather than the level of pay (the low paid are not always the poor: the poor are invariably those – individually or as a family unit – without access to work), the debate over the distribution of working time becomes keener. The widening of opportunities for access to some form of paid work assumes greater social importance and, hence, so do its facilitators and its inhibitors.

This study seeks to examine the debate over working time options by means of an analysis of preferences and innovations in the field. To try to elicit where we ought to be going from an examination of current developments and trends plus, crucially, an assessment of where people would wish to go if they had a choice – a variable not always uppermost in the thoughts of either employers or trade unions, or even government for that matter.

Project focus

1   Preferences

An area of considerable importance to the working time debate is that of working time preferences and potential trade-offs between productivity/leisure and income/leisure. The evidence – at plant and national level – appears both sketchy and inconclusive. It is widely argued, for example, that employees are becoming more willing to consider trading wages for greater leisure. If this were the case, it would obviously have major significance both in regard to the development of future working patterns and concerning employment creation. However, on closer examination these arguments and, more particularly, the evidence upon which they are based, are found to be neither clear nor conclusive. People do desire greater leisure but the link to a leisure/income trade-off is by no means apparent.

The research in this area sought to explore working time preferences within the following framework of objectives:

1   to provide data concerning the willingness or unwillingness of employees to give up part of their income for reduced hours
2   to ascertain the circumstances and conditions under which particular working time options are considered relevant and practical
3   to establish patterns of working time preferences and their relationship to time/income trade-offs
4   to isolate factors which weaken or strengthen the case for particular working time options

2   Innovations

'Time use' is of greater importance than a person's individual 'time budget'. What we do ought to be more significant than the blocks of time into which it is allocated – be it paid work, unpaid work, domestic work, leisure etc. However, to a great degree, our use of time is governed by the pattern and nature of those time 'blocks'; the divisions between working and non-working time being particularly relevant, e.g. full time workers do less domestic work than part time workers, certain full timers have longer leisure blocks than others, and the unemployed have full time 'leisure' but not the means to enjoy it. In this whole area there are innovations taking place in regard to new patterns of working time (particularly reduced working time) which have considerable bearing on the issue of 'time use'. In order to develop an understanding of time management these innovations require careful analysis and scrutiny.

Further, the way in which working time is organized has a powerful influence on employment patterns and the utilization of non-working time. Equally, it has a significant bearing on the link between work and its rewards - a major factor in the study of working time preferences and options.

There are many examples in regard to working time innovations:

1. a move from 4-crew to 5-crew shiftworking where working hours are reduced and employment created
2. major work reorganization which improves the quality of working life (e.g. by greater humanization of work or by the removal of excessive overtime)
3. reduced working time as a direct consequence of new technology bargaining
4. more flexible working time arrangements - innovations in 'flexi-time', job sharing and part time work
5. the development of annual time contracts
6. solidarity contracts
7. flexible retirement schemes
8. longer leisure blocks and provision of sabbatical or service leave.

Clearly, for reasons of time alone, detailed case study work in all these areas was not proposed. What was proposed was detailed case studies of four innovations and an examination of other developments by means of secondary sources (both nationally and internationally).

Study areas and design

The primary concern of the project was the inter-relationship between personal choice and working time innovations. In order to attempt to tease out practical rather than theoretical solutions, an element of case study work was incorporated along with an examination of policy perspectives based on trade union approaches (the JCF being a trade union based organization albeit with independent status). In addition some comment upon key factors affecting working time options into the 1990s was felt appropriate. The 'key factors' discussion is incorporated into Chapter 2, the trade union perspectives into Chapter 3 and a summary of the case study evidence is provided in Chapter 4 (the findings from other case study work are referenced and recorded at other points in this report). Chapters 5 to 8 examine key policy issues and options within the framework of the findings of the national survey on preferences conducted as part of the project. Chapter 9 seeks to draw some conclusions from the mix of survey and case study data. Before examining that data and some of the key elements which underpin it, it is perhaps necessary to air a few personal views concerning the wider subject area.

Reducing working time: some assumptions and premises

The reduction and redistribution of working time does not provide an employment panacea. It must, however, form part of the solution. Inequalities of income and wealth may be more glaring but the social differences between being employed and being unemployed have usually harsher consequences and inflict greater personal damage. The provision of choice and opportunities in employment can only be fully developed if a hard look is taken at present patterns of working time. The object should not be to provide a 'right to work', which smacks of compulsion, but to provide an opportunity to work.

It has been stated that the proponents of work redistribution base their arguments on the fallacy that there is a fixed amount of work in society at a given point in time - the 'lump of labour' or 'work fund' fallacy. This is, of course, nonsense. There is no shortage of work to be done, only the means and will to generate it. However, believing that both the means and the will are frequently variable, it is not unreasonable to propose that reorganization or redistribution might have a role to play. It is not necessary to believe that the amount of wealth in society is fixed in order to allow for a more equitable distribution - the same applies to work.

Work redistribution through working time reductions can form part of the process of employment creation, it is not the process itself. Few, if any, economists would argue that the economic levers cannot be manipulated to produce difference 'mixes' in terms of employment and unemployment. Equally few, if any, would dispute the fact that in the past particular trade-offs have been made between productivity, wages, hours and leisure. Productivity per head trebled between 1860 and 1960 and part of that gain was taken in increased leisure time. The advocates for work redistribution do not say that there is anything automatic about these processes, only that certain options do exist and some are more advantageous to employment than others.

There is a clear case for an expansion of total aggregate hours worked. The volume of work is not fixed. However, there is also a case for the development of patterns of working time which place emphasis on the reduction of individual annual working time. The two are not inconsistent; they are in fact complementary.

The key to work redistribution through reduced working time has to be choice and the encouragement of it. It ought not to be a recipe for the heavy hand of the state. There are, of course, better and worse ways of increasing choice in regard to working time. Working time should not be rationed in any strict sense but ways and means ought to be found to eliminate excessive and systematic overtime. Equally, working time options need to be broadened and greater flexibility built into existing time schedules. People who speak much of liberty and choice should encourage it.

Work expands to meet the hours allocated to it. When told 'job and finish', the rapidity of movement can be truly amazing. This is not an argument in favour of those progeny of Taylorism - the 'work study' and 'time motion' people. It is simply to note that when not shackled to the pace of a machine, the speed at which we work is dependent to a considerable degree on what we are being asked to do. If told to teach for an hour, we teach for an hour; if told to be on duty 12 hours a day, we go on duty 12 hours a day; if told to deliver so many bottles of milk to so many homes and then go home, then - minus the odd breakage - we strive to emulate Steve Cram. Quality and quantity do not always match and it is not suggested that the brain surgeon should be paid on piece-rates. Nevertheless, across a broad spectrum of jobs and occupations, people remain overly tied to the clock - prisoners of time. The time it takes - and the way that time is structured - is often as important as, if not more important than, what we actually do.

In the long term, work will be reorganized as annual working hours will almost certainly decrease and the 24-hour economy (particularly in the areas of services and leisure) will become more of a reality. However, it is argued that more may be required than an evolutionary approach. A nudge in the direction of shorter working time and the reorganization of existing work patterns might be appropriate - both in regard to providing greater opportunities for all (social policy) and to facilitate more personal choice (individual preferences). This is not to be viewed as the basis of a 'one-man one-job' charter or a recipe for excessive state regulation. What is important is that wider options are made more readily available. Many forms of working practice produce <u>prisoners of time</u>, and that is both individually and socially harmful.

Working time options need to be broadened so that the individual can be properly rewarded for his or her chosen working time preference. People need to have greater choice over the time-options available to them. They may then be freed from unnecessary work so that others can participate in it. Failing that, a certain degree of redistribution of work through time reductions may go some way to increasing the job prospects of those out of work and enhancing their prospects of some form of income. It could also do something to break down the barriers between paid employment and household work and the inequalities of opportunity which flow from it.

The study of working time preferences and innovations involves an analysis of a range of measures which could bring about reduced working time and, thereby, have social and employment spin-offs. These measures are as much, if not more, concerned with efficient production and organization as those more traditionally employed. Waiting for the clock to strike a particular hour, or avoiding work in order to build up work for the weekend, or employing people by the hour rather than allowing them greater choice over their hours, are somehow deemed acceptable where working time reductions are not. Working time options ought to be about giving people choice within a framework of real jobs, where what you do is more important than how long it takes you to do it. Certain schemes no doubt have their flaws and are of limited applicability. Equally, not all preferences should be pandered to, as much for the sake of the individual as society at large. Nevertheless, the exploration of choice within a practical framework of viable solutions - particularly those with a proven track-record - ought to form part of policy-making. This study seeks to suggest some possibilities in that direction.

Notes

1   From Bertrand Russell's <u>Roads to Freedom</u> (Allan and Unwin, London, 1918) pp. 193-4.

2 Key factors in working time reductions

Introduction

There are a number of ways in which work redistribution can be brought about – some are merely developments of existing trends (e.g. the shorter week), whilst others offer more radical solutions (e.g. job sharing). They are all concerned with the reduction of aggregate individual working time. However, they are not all the concern of this report.

Working time may be cut in three ways:

1 delaying/directing entry into the labour market;
2 reducing/redistributing/reorganizing hours for those in work;
3 encouraging/directing withdrawal from the labour market.

The discussion in this report is solely concerned with number 2. The questions of youth training, early retirement and other formulas to restrict entry into or encourage withdrawal from the labour market fall outside its focus. It is perhaps also necessary to point out that the report has a primarily British context and that it is solely concerned with paid employment in the formal economy.

Overall working hours can be reduced, essentially by four means:

Firstly, redistributing the number of jobs by forms of job sharing, job splitting or developments in part time work;
Secondly, limiting the overtime worked by those in full time

employment;

Thirdly, shortening the working week by reducing the number of hours worked, possibly in conjunction with flexi-time developments;

And fourthly, shortening the working year, either through longer holidays (including sabbaticals) or the creation of longer leisure blocks (e.g. shiftwork innovations - 12 hour shifts and 5-crew working - and the compressed (4 day) working week) or by such means as annual hours/time contracts.

All these developments have an impact on the labour supply side as well as labour demand. Effects on earnings, productivity, output and costs have to be calculated. The distribution of costs - government, employer, employee - must be weighed. Attitudes need to be assessed and the drawbacks analysed. However, in all four areas the ground is beginning to move and developments are taking place which offer the promise of wider application. These developments require careful scrutiny and examination. Equally, they need to be placed within an appropriate context. The variables involved are exhaustive, but a number of key factors, from an industrial relations perspective, may be discerned.

Productivity

Twenty-four years ago, on 1 March 1964, an American consultant, William Allen, published an article on Britain's economic performance which stirred up considerable public controversy.(1) Essentially he made 10 points:

1 There was no shortage of labour.
2 Britain had not enjoyed full employment since 1946.
3 Virtually every employee in British industry was underemployed.
4 Basic wages and salaries were too low.
5 The length of the normal working week was too long.
6 Overtime (at the time running at 12-14 per cent p.a. for male workers) was unnecessary.
7 There was a shortage of capital equipment relative to manpower.
8 Existing capital equipment was underemployed due to extensive underemployment of labour.
9 NEDO opinion that a 4 per cent growth was appropriate for Britain was wrong. The target should be increased to 8-12 per cent.
10 Britain's GNP could be produced by half the workforce - working a normal week of 35 to 40 hours and only 2-3 per cent overtime - if there was more efficient management, more flexible labour and more widespread use of new technology.

In 1988 unemployment stood at 2½ million (1964 = 370,000); there are no labour shortages as such, but serious skill shortages are widely reported in several industrial sectors and geographic areas; change has occurred in regard to new technology, labour and productivity, but the normal working week has only just dropped to below 40 hours (1987 = 39.1) and the amount of overtime worked by male manual workers is the highest for a decade. In some areas little has changed, in others everything has changed. Britain's manufacturing balance of payments has worsened, unemployment has become a permanent social feature, but working hours remain obstinately static (in terms of actual hours worked they have increased in recent years).

Changes in working time will not, of themselves, bring about economic growth and fuller employment. However, as Allen suggested, they are a necessary prerequisite for the attainment of a high wage/high productivity economy and they are - as will be argued elsewhere in this report - an important adjunct to any manpower strategy. There are also, of course, important social reasons why the barriers to reduced working time and new patterns of work need to be broken down and individuals freed from the artificial time constraints that too often govern their working lives.

The mainstream economic debate has changed radically since the 1960s - not least affected by changes in fiscal and government policies - but, it could be argued, primarily influenced by external forces unforeseeable twenty years ago:

- the effect of the 1973 five-fold increase in oil prices;
- the impact of the discovery of North Sea oil on the U.K. balance of trade;
- the shake-out of jobs in manufacturing industry as a consequence of world-wide recession;
- the advent of new technology.

These and other forces have combined, in a sense, to 'solve' the familiar productivity problem in manufacturing, whilst leaving in their wake permanent unemployment and greater social division. See Figures 2.1 and 2.2.

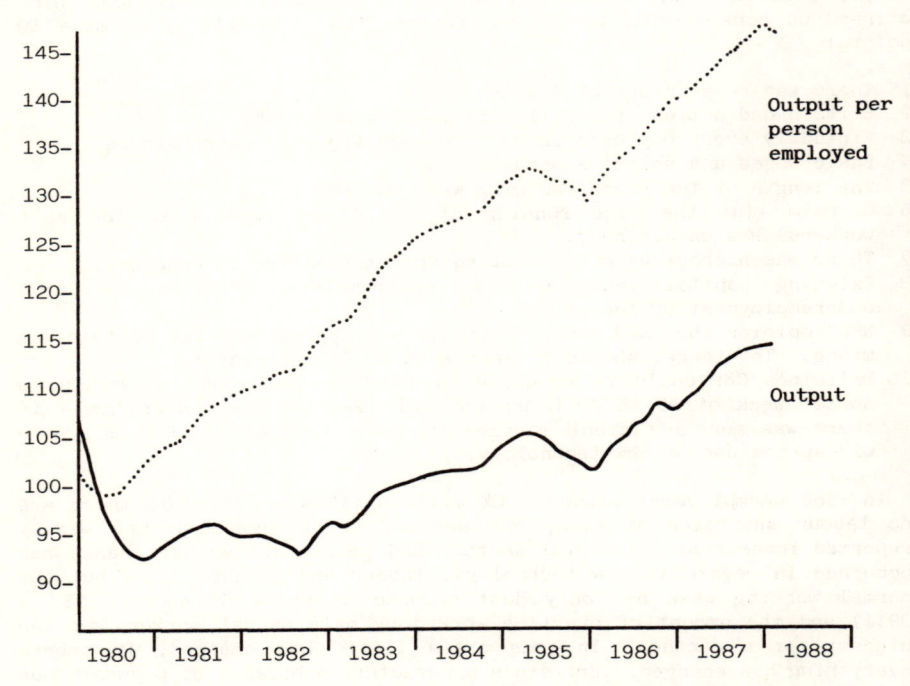

Figure 2.1   Output and productivity - manufacturing industries (SIC 1980)

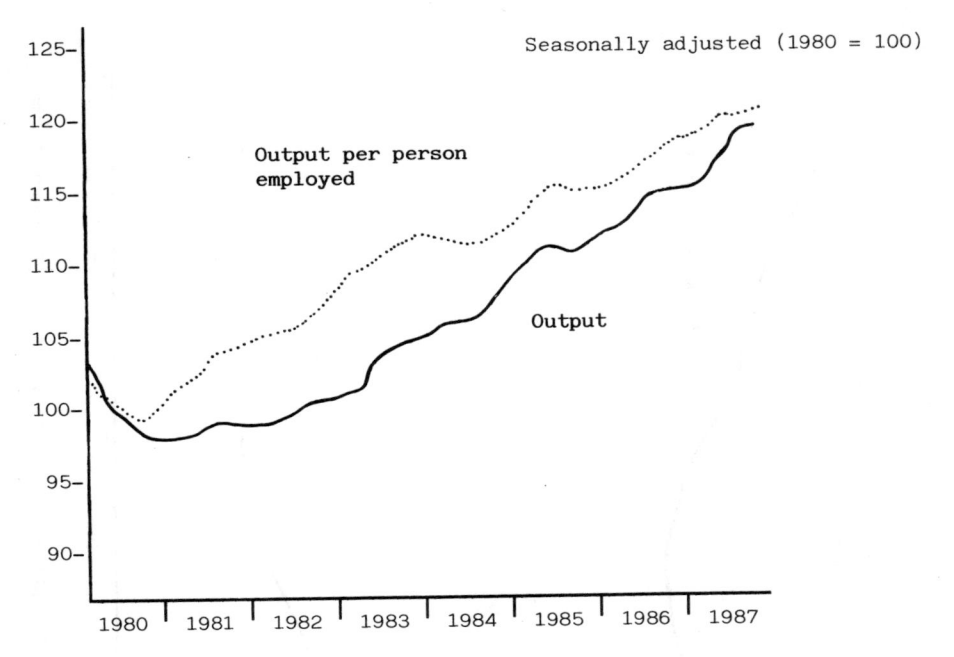

Figure 2.2 Output and productivity - whole economy

Source: Department of Employment Gazette (July 1988)

Output per person in manufacturing signifies a new international competitivenes, but reduced output points to the converse of a net loss in manufacturing trade (probably for the first time since the industrial evolution). The 1979-81 fall in output characterized two million jobs which disappeared in the manufacturing sector of the British economy.

Occupational changes

Employment changes to the manufacturing and non-manufacturing sectors are simply illustrated in Figure 2.3.

However, behind these more recent developments is an ongoing movement between manufacturing and the service sectors which, if the experience of the United States is a good guide, has a degree of historical inevitability about it. This is reflected in occupational changes which were occurring long before the 1980-81 recession - see Table 2.1.

Since 1981 further adjustments have taken place which have bolstered the service sector of the economy - see Table 2.2.

These changes have significant implications for the future labour market. A recent review of the economy and of employment prospects to 1995 makes some interesting predictions about the changing composition of the labour force.(2)

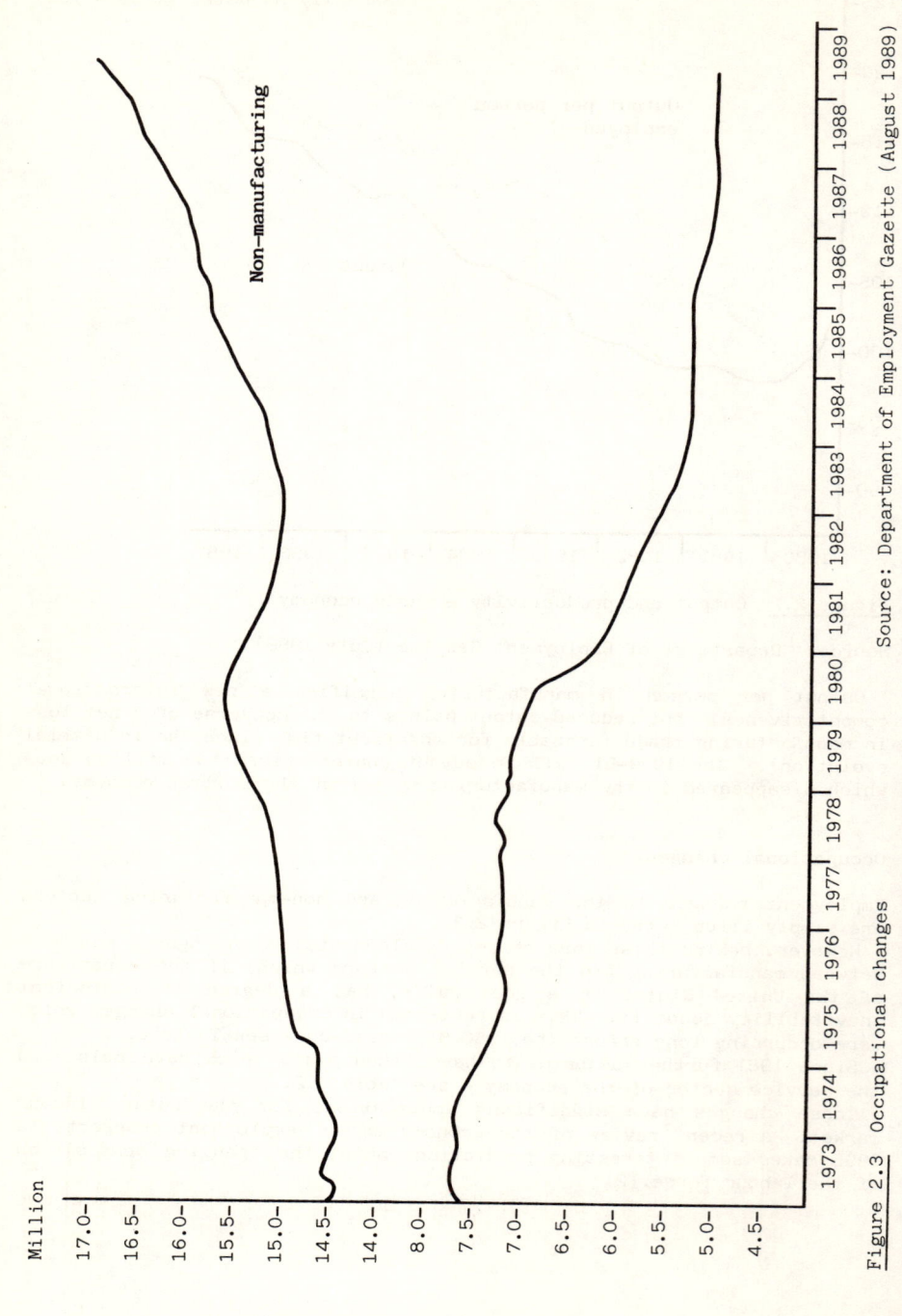

Figure 2.3 Occupational changes

Source: Department of Employment Gazette (August 1989)

Table 2.1
Occupational change (1971-81)

	1971 Males	1971 Females	1971 Total	1981 Males	1981 Females	1981 Total	% change Males	% change Females	% change Persons
Managerial and administration									
1 Managers and administrators	532	23	555	650	56	706	+22	+44	+27
10 Sales representatives	370	45	415	311	54	365	-16	+19	-12
20 Skilled personal service	1,226	811	2,037	1,234	894	2,128	1	+10	+5
Higher level service									
2 Education professions	321	383	703	381	482	863	+19	+26	+23
3 Health and welfare	119	457	656	250	705	955	+25	+54	+46
4 Other professions	706	123	829	776	221	997	+10	+80	+20
5 Literary, artistic, sports	100	51	151	106	73	179	+5	+45	+19
Higher level industrial									
6 Engineers, scientists	442	8	451	546	32	578	+23	+282	+28
7 Technicians, draughtsmen	476	38	514	480	63	543	+1	+65	+6
Lower level service and supervisory									
8 Clerical occupations	925	1,660	2,584	730	1,808	2,538	-21	+9	-2
9 Secretarial occupations	6	826	832	17	861	877	+161	+4	+5
11 Other sales occupations	274	815	1,089	223	811	1,034	-18	-1	-5
12 Supervisors	114	99	213	131	165	295	+15	+66	+39
21 Other personal services	328	1,447	1,755	301	1,478	1,779	-8	+2	0
Craft/foremen									
13 Foremen	509	42	551	498	46	544	-2	+10	-1
14 Engineering craft occupations	1,873	43	1,916	1,691	33	1,724	-10	-23	-10
15 Construction craft occupations	809	3	812	755	7	762	-7	+131	-6
16 Other craft occupations	335	56	391	250	32	282	-25	-44	-2
Lower level industrial and others									
17 Skilled operatives	442	408	851	352	291	643	-20	-29	-24
18 Other operatives	3,612	1,155	4,767	2,937	845	3,782	-19	-27	-21
19 Security occupations	212	17	229	246	37	283	+16	+115	+23
22 Other occupations	882	55	937	557	46	603	-37	-17	-36
24 Inadequately described	98	125	223	109	97	205	+11	-23	-8
All in employment	14,791	8,690	23,481	13,531	9,134	22,665	+5	-3	

Source: MSC (1985 Internal) Occupational Change 1971-1981 (Table A2)

Table 2.2
Comparison of employees in employment via standard industrial classification

SIC 1980, Great Britain, Seasonally adjusted (000s), Figures for June each year	1982	1983	1984	1985	1986	1987
Manufacturing	5,761	5,430	5,315	5,272	5,151	5,085
% of total	27.6	26.4	25.6	25.1	24.4	23.8
Production and construction	7,470	7,086	6,936	6,852	6,654	6,569
% of total	35.7	34.5	33.5	32.6	31.5	30.7
Services	13,078	13,130	13,466	13,821	14,127	14,493
% of total	62.3	63.9	65.0	65.8	67.0	67.8
All employees	20,896	20,556	20,731	21,003	21,100	21,372

N.B. Manufacturing   = SIC 2-4
     Production & construction = SIC 1-5
     Services   = SIC 6-9
     All employees   = SIC 0-9

Source: Department of Employment Gazette, January 1988, Table 1.2

Throughout the economy, employment is expected to grow by about 0.5 per cent per year, producing a little over two million new jobs by 1995. 70 per cent of this job growth (1.4 million) will be in the business and miscellaneous services sectors, which are predicted to grow in terms of numbers employed by between 3½ and 4 per cent per year. The nature of the organization of work in these sectors indicates that part time working will continue to increase disproportionately, as it has done over the last decade, so that part timers, who constituted 21 per cent of the workforce in 1981 and 23.3 per cent in 1986, will make up 28 per cent of all employees by 1995. This will have a further spin-off effect on the number of female employees, since 90 per cent of part time jobs are taken up by women, who will form half of all employees by the middle of the next decade when there will be one million more women in employment. This is a growth twice the size of the projected increase in the female labour force by 1995. In comparison, in June 1987 there were 9,874,000 female employees in the United Kingdom, which represented 45 per cent of the total.

Other economic sectors predicted to experience a growth in jobs to 1995 are non-marketed services, such as education, health and public administration (up by 100,000), construction (up by 170,000), and distribution and transport (up by 340,000), while those experiencing a decline are manufacturing (down by 500,000 - despite a projected growth in productivity of 4.5 per cent per year between now and 1990), and primary and utilities, such as North Seal oil, gas and mining (down by 100,000). Overall, therefore, 1.14 million new jobs will be created, although the review predicts this will have only a minor impact on the unemployment figures by bringing them down first to 2.8 million by 1990 and 2.5 million by 1995. At the time of the publication of the review (September 1987), unemployment stood at 2.9 million and has since fallen further to 2.7 million (Department of Employment figures).

Occupationally, the only group of workers to experience a net decrease in employment is the semi- and unskilled labourers (down 500,000). Net increases, on the other hand, are forecasted for craft and skilled workers (up 150,000), clerical and secretarial (up 225,000), sales and personal services (up 300,000), managerial (up 400,000), and professional and related occupations (up 825,000). The percentage share of the labour market of each of these groups now and in 1995 is shown in Table 2.3.

Table 2.3
Occupational employment 1986-1995 (% shares)

Group	1986	1995
Semi and unskilled labourers	19.6	16.4
Craft and skilled workers	13.2	13.1
Clerical and secretarial	15.4	15.4
Sales and personal services	17.9	18.0
Managerial	13.8	14.6
Professional and related	20.3	22.5

Industrial relations

British industrial relations has undergone a sea-change in the 1980s. A combination of economic recession and government legislation has placed trade unions on the defensive and swung the balance of power at the workplace firmly onto the side of management. Many firms and organizations either have been forced into work reorganization (as a consequence of rationalization, closures, etc) or have elected to make alterations in their working practices, often as a result of or in tandem with technological change. The scale of these changes at the workplace differs across sectors and there is an academic debate as to how radical and deep-seated they have been. Nevertheless, few involved in industrial relations over the past nine years would fail to agree that there have been marked changes in practice since the 1970s and most of us do not expect the 1970s ever to return.(3) A number of features are worth recording.

Industrial action, with the exception of one or two notable disputes in the public sector (particularly that in coal in 1984/5) has dropped dramatically, although there are some indications that work stoppages may be rising again - see Table 2.4.

Membership of trade unions has fallen, which has had a knock-on effect on finances and militancy - see Table 2.5.

Other noteworthy developments have been:

- particular reduction in trade union 'heartlands'
- high level of mergers, transfers and amalgamations
- high level of competition for membership
- more emphasis on 'open' unionism i.e. less industry-specific or 'craft' oriented
- traditional links with locations less important
- highest ever proportion of women in unions
- public sector unionism now more than half of total
- inter-union squabbling (e.g. over Wapping and single union deals), culminating in the EETPU's suspension and expulsion from the TUC.

Table 2.4
Britain's strike record: stoppages in progress 1967-1988

Year	Working days lost (thousands)	Working days lost per 1,000 employees*	Workers involved (thousands)	Stoppages
1967	2,787	122	734	2,133
1968	4,690	207	2,258	2,390
1969	6,846	303	1,665	3,146
1970	10,980	489	1,801	3,943
1971	13,551	612	1,178	2,263
1972	23,909	1,080	1,734	2,530
1973	7,197	317	1,528	2,902
1974	14,750	647	1,626	2,946
1975	6,012	265	809	2,332
1976	3,284	146	668	2,034
1977	10,142	448	1,166	2,737
1978	9,405	413	1,041	2,498
1979	29,474	1,273	4,608	2,125
1980	11,964	521	834	1,348
1981	4,266	195	1,513	1,344
1982	5,313	248	2,103	1,538
1983	3,754	178	574	1,364
1984	27,135	1,278	1,464	1,221
1985	6,402	298	791	903
1986	1,920	89	720	1,074
1987	3,546	163	887	1,016
1988	3,702	164	790	781

*Based on the latest available mid-year (June) estimates of employees in employment. Source: Employment Gazette (July 1989)

Table 2.5
Membership trends in largest TUC unions: 1979-1987

Union	31.12.78	31.12.86		Change (1979-87) %	Change (1986-87) %
TGWU	2,072,818	1,377,944	(1)	-34	(-3.9)
AEU	1,199,465	857,559	(2)	-29	(-12.0)
GMB	964,836	814,084	(3)	-16	(-3.1)
NALGO	769,405	750,430	(4)	-2	(-0.2)
NUPE	712,392	657,633	(5)	-8	(0.9)
ASTMS	471,000	390,000	(6)	-17	(-)
USDAW	462,178	381,984	(7)	-17	(-1.0)
EETPU	420,000	336,155	(8)	-20	(-3.3)
UCATT	320,723	249,485	(9)	-22	(+0.3)
NUT	291,239	154,455	(14)	-37	(-11.3)
NUM	254,887	104,941	(-)	-59	(-22.4)
CPSA	224,780	150,514	(17)	-33	(+2.7)
COHSE	215,033	212,312	(11)	-1	(-0.3)
SOGAT	203,352	199,594	(12)	-2	(-3.1)
TASS	200,954	241,000	(10)	+20	(-4.1)
UCW	197,157	191,959	(13)	-3	(-1.2)
NUR	180,000	125,000	(19)	-31	(-4.0)
APEX	151,343	83,614	(-)	-45	n/a
BIFU	126,343	158,746	(15)	+26	(+0.8)
NCU	121,406	155,643	(16)	+28	(-3.5)
NUTGW	116,095	75,063	(-)	-35	n/a
NAS/UWT	111,566	123,945	(20)	+11	(-2.9)
NGA	109,904	125,587	(18)	+14	(-0.4)
ISTC	106,955	68,000	(-)	-36	n/a
Total TUC	12,128,178	9,243,297		-24	(-3.6)

15

The cumulative effect has been to erode trade union influence both with government and in the collective bargaining arena. At plant and workplace level a dramatic loss of influence has not occurred – derecognition is a rare phenomenon – but few would argue that the balance of power around the negotiating table has not measurably shifted. Developments which might be highlighted would include:

1. a limit to the extension of collective bargaining
2. a rekindling of interest in consultation schemes, particularly 'works councils'
3. 'positive employment relations' policies – to win 'hearts and minds'
4. some bypassing of union networks
5. decentralization of bargaining structures – relating pay to performance at plant/departmental level
6. movement towards harmonization of terms
7. the use of package deals – variations on 'productivity deals'
8. greater length of settlement – longer wage deals
9. linking of performance to pay and pay to profit, including profit-sharing
10. considerable emphasis on 'flexibility'
11. some 'minimum dislocation' clauses – 'no strike' deals
12. greater provision for third party intervention – arbitration
13. increased distinction of different types of employment contract – 'core' and 'peripheral'
14. a growth of single union deals
15. the spread of profit sharing and share ownership schemes fuelled by government incentives and the privatization programme.

Again, whether by 'macho management', decentralized bargaining or the simple reassertion of managerial prerogatives, the overall trend of the 1980s has been away from trade union corporatism and towards the flowering of managerial-led, individual company systems which seek to emphasize organizational loyalty. This has had a considerable influence over work reorganization, particularly in the wake of new technology. It also has had and will have powerful implications for the debate over working time.

Labour market: the 'flexible firm'

Much has been written about the emergence of the 'flexible firm' based on the model developed at the Institute of Manpower Studies at Sussex University (4) – see Figure 2.4.

Flexibility can be seen to operate at a number of levels, including that of working time and working patterns:

```
Functional    - job flexibility
                cross-traded craftsmen
                multi-skilling
                skill transfer
                simplified grading

Operational   - shiftwork innovations
                longer leisure blocks
                annual time contracts
                flexi-time
                overtime
```

Structural - 'core' and 'peripheral'
          sub-contracting
          self-employed
          part time
          temporary work
          youth trainees - YTS/JTS
          government schemes - CP
          outsourcing - homeworking/networking

	Self employment	
	First peripheral group Secondary labour market Numerical flexibility	
Agency temporaries	**Core group** Primary labour market Functional flexibility	Sub contracting
Second peripheral group					
Short term contracts	Public subsidy trainees	Delayed recruitment	Job sharing	Part time
	Increased outsourcing	

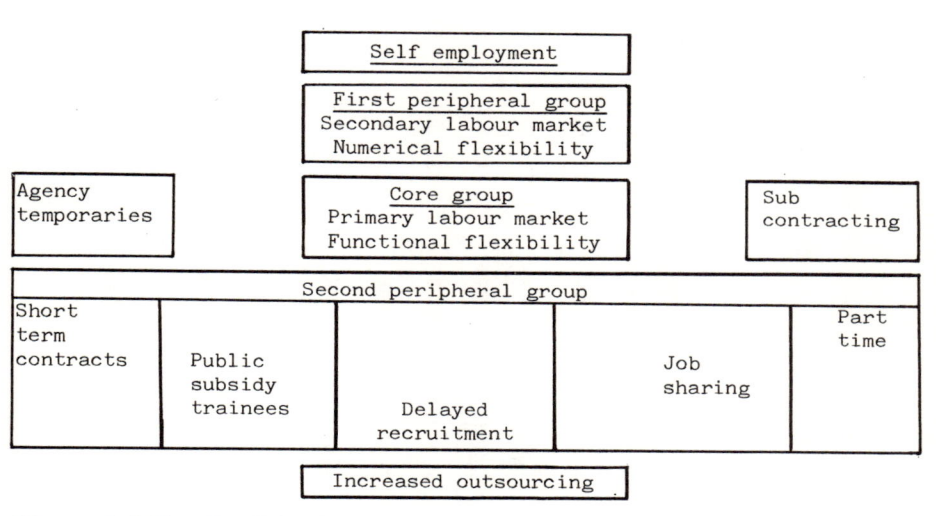

Figure 2.4 The flexible firm
Source: Institute of Manpower Studies

Without necessarily embracing the 'flexible firm' concept, it is clear that labour market changes and manpower strategies have had a profound impact on work organization.

The debate over labour flexibility has caused considerable controversy in the United Kingdom.(5) The extent to which firms are opting for more functional flexibility in regard to individual jobs and numerical flexibility in regard to working patterns - such as greater use of temporary workers, part timers, sub-contracting and the self-employed - is hotly contended.(6) Matters such as what makes a part time workforce more flexible than a full time workforce are also at stake. Nevertheless, whilst the issue of how radical and how extensive the increase in 'labour flexibility' has become is open to question, few would dispute the fact that certain elements in the equation are on the increase (e.g. part time work, sub-contracting, temporary work and the self-employed) and most aspects of it are unlikely to go away. The pace and significance of change might be queried, but the direction of change ought not to be in doubt.(7)

A recent Department of Employment study depicted the 'flexible workforce' in terms of those doing part time or temporary work plus the self-employed.(8) Regardless of the adequacy of such a definition, the study did illustrate both the industrial distribution and variations in working patterns and placed some figures on the cross-over between these types of 'flexibility' - see Table 2.6 and Figure 2.5.

Table 2.6

Industrial distribution of the flexible workforce, Great Britain, 1986

	Traditional workforce: permanent full time		Flexible workforce: all other workers		Total in employment
0 Agriculture	202,100	40%	302,700	60%	504,800
1 Energy and water supply	575,500	94%	34,400	6%	609,800
2 Chemicals and minerals: extraction and manufacture	723,400	91%	71,200	9%	794,600
3 Metal goods, engineering and vehicles	2,283,500	90%	256,600	10%	2,540,100
4 Other manufacturing	1,932,000	81%	462,900	19%	2,394,900
5 Construction	963,600	58%	711,600	42%	1,675,200
6 Distribution, hotels and catering, repairs	2,257,400	48%	2,429,900	52%	4,687,300
7 Transport and communication	1,199,100	85%	218,400	15%	1,417,600
8 Insurance, financial and business services	1,618,300	72%	640,400	28%	2,258,600
9 Other services (professional and scientific, public administration, etc)	3,808,300	58%	2,704,300	42%	6,512,600
Workplace outside U.K.	12,400	62%	7,500	38%	20,000
Inadequately described	16,700	64%	9,400	36%	26,100
Total – all industries	15,592,300	66%	7,849,300	34%	23,441,600

All temporary 1,621 625 97 2,189 **All self-employed 2,727** 115 784 326 3,914 **All part-time 5,139**

<u>Figure 2.5</u> Overlaps between the three main categories of flexible worker, as shown in the 1986 LFS

The study further noted the growth in part time employment in the United Kingdom (of which 90 per cent is female) and used data to make comparisons between the 'flexible workforce' (or perhaps more accurately the non-permanent, non-full time employee workforce) in the UK and Europe and that in the United States – see Tables 2.7, 2.8 and 2.9.

<u>Table 2.7</u>
The growth of part time work in Great Britain, 1951-87

Thousands and per cent

	Total in employment	Full time employment	Part time employment	Part time as per cent of all employment
1951	22,135	21,304	831	4%
1961	23,339	21,272	2,066	9%
1971	23,733	19,828	3,904	16%
1981(A)	22,881	18,977	3,905	17%
1981(B)	23,754	18,871	4,883	21%
1987	24,229	18,646	5,583	23%

Note: 1981 change of definition

Table 2.8
International comparisons: The European Community, 1985 (%)

	Men in employment		Women in employment		All in employment	
	Full time permanent employees	All other workers	Full time permanent employees	All other workers	Full time permanent employees	All other workers
Luxembourg	85	15	72	28	80	20
France	76	24	64	36	71	29
Belgium	76	24	56	44	69	31
West Germany	78	22	54	46	69	31
Ireland	66	34	70	30	67	33
Italy	66	34	65	35	66	34
United Kingdom	78	22	49	51	66	34
Netherlands	77	23	40	60	64	36
Denmark	69	31	43	57	57	43
Greece	40	60	35	65	38	62
European Community	73	27	55	45	67	33

Source: Spring 1985 Labour Force Survey

Table 2.9
Trends in full time year round work in the USA labour force, 1974-85

Proportion (per cent) of those who worked during the year who worked full time year round

	Men	Women	White	Black	Hispanic	All
1974	64.6	40.4	55.0	49.6		54.4
1976	64.2	41.1	54.7	51.4	50.3	54.3
1978	66.3	43.7	56.8	52.5	53.8	56.4
1980	65.2	44.7	56.5	52.7	53.1	56.1
1982	62.3	45.9	55.3	52.3	52.5	55.0
1984	66.5	48.2	58.3	67.3	47.3	58.1
1985	66.8	48.9	58.8	67.6	48.1	58.7

Source: Current population survey - March supplement on work experience as reported periodically in Monthly Labor Review

From this somewhat general data it could be argued that the 'core' workforce operates at similar levels in the United Kingdom as in the United States: one-third of males and about half of females falling into the 'flexible' workforce category. part time work has clearly expanded in the UK as has temporary work in the United States.9 Data is patchy but a British employers' survey among 700 member companies of the CBI (Confederation of British Industry) in late 1984 showed an expectation of an increase in certain areas and this expectation was particularly strong among major employers see Table 2.10

Thus, the trend towards a larger 'flexible' workforce is real in a certain number of senses, which does have implications for working patterns and hours. It is likely that there will be increased opportunities in the part time and temporary employment sectors, which may or may not stimulate variations in hours and options. It is also likely that patterns of work, e.g. shiftworking, will alter to meet the needs of a 24-hour service economy and a technologically-driven society.(10)

All of these changes will affect some before others. From the industrial distribution in the United Kingdom it is clear that part time work (the major constituent part of the 'flexible' workforce) is already well established in distribution, hotels, catering, etc and in the service sector in general. The extent to which this element of the workforce is able to influence the drive for new working patterns and wider employee preferences on hours is questionable. It is usually assumed that part time and temporary workers are the most poorly organized and in the weakest position in regard to negotiating terms and conditions. However, it could be argued that its growth in size represents a wider range of options in themselves and that the less work is thought of in terms of full time, permanent employees, the more likely it is that a greater choice of hours will become available to more people. Whatever the argument, an assumption that the debate over working hours should focus solely on full time employees (a trap that trade unions too often fall into) should not be countenanced in the late 1980s.

Table 2.10
Expanding use of flexible workforce 1985-1989

Per cent

	Manufacturing industries	Other industries	All employers	Employers with 5,000+ employees
Net proportion of employers expecting an increase against those expecting a decrease in:				
the proportion of part timers	+8	+15	+13	+26
the proportion of temporary workers	+17	+6	+13	+17
the extent of shift-working	+32	+10	+24	+25
the extent of contracted out activities	+29	+21	+24	+43

Working time trends and developments

There is an historical tendency for reduced working hours traceable from the nineteenth century. It has been argued on the basis of overall data that this trend operates at around 10 per cent every decade in regard to lifetime hours of work.(11) What is perhaps surprising, given the enormous pressure to reduce hours and the number of settlements which appear to reduce the normal working week, is that the current trend in actual weekly hours worked of both male and female workers (across occupational boundaries) in the United Kingdom during the 1980s has been <u>upwards</u> rather than downward. This is perhaps best illustrated by the figures for full time male manual workers, normally regarded as the pacesetters in reduced hours - see Table 2.11 and Figure 2.6.

Table 2.11
Actual hours of full time male manual workers (selected years)

1951 - 47.9
1961 - 47.9
1971 - 44.7
1981 - 43.5
1982 - 43.9
1983 - 43.6
1984 - 44.4
1985 - 44.6
1986 - 44.5
1987 - 44.7

Source: Department of Employment Gazette, March 1988

A major factor in this lengthening of hours has been the increase in overtime working. Average overtime hours of operatives in manufacturing industry of those who actually work overtime has increased on a weekly basis from 8.2 hours in 1981 to 9.3 hours in 1987.

Thus, some reductions in the working week are being negotiated, albeit fewer in the last few years than in the earlier part of the 1980s, but their impact is being negated by increased overtime. It will be argued more fully later that this process has been assisted by trade unions placing all their reduced hours eggs in one basket - the shorter working week - to the detriment of other working time options (see Chapter 3).(13) Consequently, much of the force behind the moral argument that shorter hours will help the unemployed is taken away by the knowledge that the shorter normal working week has had little or no impact on reducing working hours overall.(14)

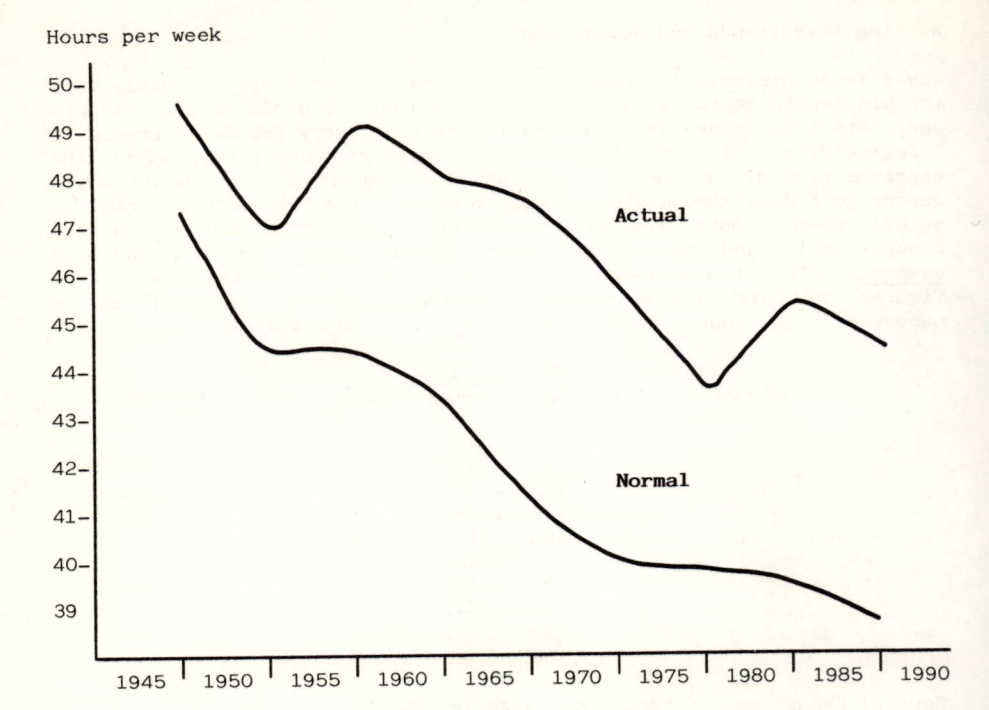

Figure 2.6 Normal and actual weekly hours of male manual workers 1945-1988

Source: A. Evans and S. Palmer - Negotiating Shorter Working Hours p.16 and Department of Employment Gazette

If the shorter working week has given little cause for comfort to the supporters of reduced hours, there have been changes in other areas which might indicate a more positive trend. Holidays have been a significant area of reduction - see Table 2.12.

Table 2.12

Holidays with pay - Percentage of manual employees with basic (i.e. additional to public and customary) holidays of:

	3 weeks	Between 3 and 4 weeks	4 weeks	Between 4 and 5 weeks	5 weeks	5 weeks and over
1980	2	4	19	19	55	0
1981	0	2	11	25	61	1
1982	0	2	5	21	61	1
1983	0	0	5	17	60	18
1984	0	0	5	15	61	19
1985	0	0	1	16	63	20
1986	0	0	0	14	63	23

Source: Employment Gazette March 1987

In addition to holidays, the working lifetime is being thinned at either end with delayed recruitment into the labour market for the young (the two-year Youth Training Scheme - YTS - and other more recent measures encouraging an 18 plus entry rather than at 16, the legal minimum) and much greater use of early retirement for those approaching the end of their working lives. Other initiatives of interest are the greater use of flexi-time arrangements (particularly among office workers), the extension of shiftworking (including a trend towards longer shifts plus longer 'leisure blocks' - 9,10 and 12 hour shifts or days effectively compressing the work week to 3 or 4 blocks of working time), the use of weekend working (Goodyear Tyres has recently announced a further 286 weekend jobs, working two 12-hour shifts, at a plant already having some 374 such weekend workers) and a movement towards annual hours systems (payment on the basis of a contract to do so many hours a year, with high and low-periods - occasionally seasonal - rather than the traditional weekly hours contract).(15) These developments will be studied later in association with the employee preference survey (see, particularly, Chapters 5-8)

Not all of these innovations will automatically reduce hours. Not all are as widespread as case study evidence would occasionally indicate (a few radical innovations often get a lot of publicity and talked about as though significant sections of industry were about to or were following suit). Nevertheless, there are grounds for believing that employers are becoming more prepared to seek solutions which fit their individual circumstances and needs rather than being tied to traditional practices. What is perhaps of greater importance is that employees are willing to see the utility of different patterns and make conscious decisions to pursue a particular option in preference to one or more others.(16) Choice is seldom if ever total, but there are few cases where work is concerned of which that is true anyway.

Summary

The key factors raised in this chapter - productivity, occupational changes, industrial relations, the labour market and trends in working time - by no means represent an exhaustive list. However, they are issues which will recur throughout this report as trade union perspectives, case study evidence, survey data and a range of working time developments/innovations are explored in greater detail. The trade union perspective, which is the subject of the next chapter, is an important area of concern - not only because it has such a vital bearing on the working time debate but also because the origins of this study lay in a particular understanding of the failures of the trade union movement in general to successfully address the question in its totality. In so doing, it is argued, an opportunity has been missed and the direction of change has been little influenced; perhaps to the extent that the initiative now lies elsewhere - with managers and with employees - both to the good and to the bad. To try to understand what this means for future policy options and directions, a more detailed analysis of the trade union role is required.

Notes

1. Cited in Michael Shanks - 'The Innovators' (Penguin, Hammondsworth, Middlesex, 1967) pp. 34-37.
2. Review of the Economy and Employment 1987. Institute of Employment Research, Warwick University, 1987.
3. For a useful survey of industrial relations changes in the early 1980s see C. Brewster and S. Connock - Industrial relations: cost-effective strategies (Hutchinson, London, 1985), which includes a section on initiatives in working time.
4. An up-date of that research model and some critical observations in regard to 'flexibility' are to be found in J. Atkinson and N. Meager - 'Is flexibility just a flash in the pan?' Personnel Management, September 1986 pp 26-29
5. A debate which is usually credited as being initiated by the work into the 'flexible firm' of the Institute of Manpower Studies at Sussex University. See, for example, J. Atkinson - 'New patterns of working relationships' (IMS Sussex University, 1984) and 'Manning for uncertainty - some emerging U.K. work patterns' (IMS, 1984).
6. See, for example, J. MacInnes - Thatcherism at Work (Open University Press, Milton Keynes, 1987 pp. 113-124).
7. For a survey of flexibility cases see C. Curson (ed.) - Flexible patterns of work (Institute of Personnel Management, London, 1986).
8. The remaining tables in this section of the paper are all taken from this Department of Employment study by Catherine Hakim - 'Trends in the flexible workforce', Employment Gazette, November 1987, pp. 549-560.
9. For further international comparisons and analysis of working time developments see P. Blyton - 'Changes in working time: an international review' (Croom Helm, London, 1985).
10. For a wider discussion of these and other issues in the future of work debate see:
    C. Handy - The future of work (Blackwell, Oxford, 1984)
    D. Clutterbuck and R. Hill - The remaking of work (Grant McIntyre, London, 1981)
    B. Sherman and C. Jenkins - The collapse of work (Eyre Methuen, London, 1979)
    A. Gorz - Farewell to the working class (Pluto Press, London, 1982)
    C. Leadbetter and J. Lloyd - In search of work (Penguin Books, Hammonsworth, Middlesex, 1987).
11. See, for example, P. Armstrong - Technical changes and reductions in life hours of work (Technical Change Centre, London, 1984).
12. Consequently the impact on unemployment has been marginal. A conclusion also drawn by R.A. Hart - Shorter working time: a dilemma for collective bargaining (OECD, Paris 1984).
13. See also Paul Rathkey - 'Trade unions, collective bargaining and reduced working time: a critical assessment', Employee Relations Vol. 8 No. 1 1986 pp. 4-9.
14. An excellent analysis of the problems of reducing working time is to be found in Rolande Cuvillier - The reduction of working time (ILO, Geneva, 1984) and for a practical negotiators' guide see A. Evans and S. Palmer - Negotiating shorter working hours (Macmillan, London, 1985).

15. Many of the studies listed in these references examine such innovations. For an overall analysis see Paul Rathkey – <u>Work and the prisoners of time</u> (Work and Society Report No. 11, Institute of Manpower Studies, Sussex University, 1984).
    Also for case studies in new working patterns see: Paul Rathkey – <u>Work Sharing and the reduction and re-organization of work at firm level</u> (EEC, Brussels, 1985).
16. The evidence is limited by the case study data and the small number of employers who are prepared to offer choice. However, in chemicals, oil refining and canning, there are trends towards employee preferences for longer shifts (and hence longer blocks of leisure) and some indication that the same is true of annual hours systems.

3 Trade unions, collective bargaining, flexibility and reduced working time

Introduction

Rising unemployment in the 1970s and particularly during the period 1979-82 focused trade union strategies on the question of job creation. The initial response was largely a restatement of Keynesian macro-economic policies plus a series of short term 'special measures'.(1) The deepening of the recession in the early 80s caused a minor re-think and an examination of notions of work redistribution.(2) The immediate solution was seen as 'the shorter working week' and, despite a growing awareness of other options, this remains the cornerstone of TUC thinking and that of its major affiliates.(3)

In this chapter, the intention is to examine the development of the trade union approach to working time, assess its successes and failures, and seek an understanding of the movement towards reduced working time. From that assessment, it is argued that prevailing strategies are unlikely to bear dividends in terms of their own objectives – the reduction of unemployment. If work reorganization and new patterns of working time are to assist the unemployed, a more radical approach is called for by all major parties concerned – employers, trade unions and government. Effectively, this requires a new approach to the bargaining of reduced working time.

The TUC and shorter working time

A fairly uncompromising stance has been taken by the TUC which has been campaigning for a shorter working week with no compensatory reductions in pay whatsoever. The 1984 Congress resolution, for example talks of:

> ... a reduction in the working week to 35 hours, without loss of pay ... as a first step towards a further substantial reduction in the working week.

Reduced working time has traditionally been the subject of 'free' collective bargaining, and trade unions have been suspicious of any encroachments on 'voluntarism'. Britain's trade unions, unlike their European counterparts, have been reluctant to seek legislation on hours or annual holidays.(4)

The TUC began actively to campaign for shorter working time in 1979. Despite what the TUC sees as encouraging signs, there seems little or no progress towards substantially reducing overtime, indeed, in some sectors, it has marginally increased.(5) Equally, the shorter working week has had little impact on individual annual working time apart from where the recession has reduced overtime opportunities. Recently, fewer employers appear to be conceding hours reductions, although they remain a regular feature of union claims.(6)

The TUC's 'campaign for reduced working time', for all its information, check-lists and good advice, has largely suffered from a lack of clear direction. In 1981, the TUC passed a resolution which argued (among other things):

> Congress believes that a radical new initiative is required in the area of annual working hours.
>
> It draws attention to the legislative provisions in a number of EEC countries, restricting by law the number of hours worked per year, and to the superior holiday provisions existing in many of those countries.
>
> Congress instructs the General Council to give urgent consideration to the question of the introduction of a policy for all unions which will limit the number of hours worked annually, reduce the working week by statute to a maximum of 35 hours, provide for a minimum holiday entitlement of six weeks per annum, plus sabbatical leave after a stipulated number of years for all employees and reduce the qualifying age for retirement pensions to 60 years.

This was more than a litany of desired ends; it actually urged the General Council (rather than the Government) to formulate a policy which, among other things, would 'reduce the working week by statute' and cited European legislation in support of its case. By the following year, this 'radical new initiative' had disappeared among the member unions' own lack of consensus on the matter. No clear-cut legislative proposals emerged and the TUC's lack of conviction was encapsulated by its reference to discussions 'with a future sympathetic Government' (read Labour Government - circa 1991/92?).

The 1983 TUC Congress once again passed a motion on working hours. It called for a study to establish best practices, both in Britain and abroad, and discussions with the Labour Party in regard to a legislative policy for shortening the working week. Overtime and the working year were to be left to collective bargaining. The 1984 Congress reversed this line and argued for a legal limit to be placed on 'weekly' overtime working, though what that limit was, was not specified. This advocacy of a weekly limit was despite the fact that the European evidence on overtime restrictions (such as in France, Belgium and Scandinavia) pointed clearly to the need for longer periods to be considered e.g. for quarterly and annual limits. It also demanded a 35-hour week without loss of earnings, six weeks annual holiday, a phased reduction in the working week for those over 55 (also without loss of earnings) and a movement to reducing the retiring age to 55. The resolution, however, recognized that this set of demands might not be applied immediately and called for talks with the Labour Party on how 'planned national initiatives' (legislation?) could be 'pursued by the next Labour Government'. Congress's initiatives on working time appeared to be totally subsumed within its overall 'PLG' strategy - Pray for a Labour Government!

The TUC's problems in formulating a firm policy on working time which might have practical implications in the here and now exemplifies the different, often conflicting, views held on the subject by its member unions. It has felt unable to specify overtime targets; it has ignored the concept of annual working time; it has had little to say about shift-work innovations and has remained silent on job sharing.(7) It has repeatedly urged action on overtime, but has only recently decided that legislation is necessary and the current parameters of that proposed legislation are so lax and vague as to seriously question the intentions and commitment of its framers.(8) The overall policy is kept afloat by repeated calls for a 35-hour week with, apparently, little questioning of whether the shorter working week is the best road to achieve reductions in annual working time despite the TUC's own acknowledgement that cuts in weekly working time have rarely resulted in increased employment levels.(9)

The future direction of British trade unions in regard to reduced working time remains largely obscure beyond being in favour of the idea, having little notion of what that might mean in practice and waiting for a future Labour Government to play the role of the Seventh Cavalry! Meanwhile, at shop-floor level, bargains and trade-offs are being struck which could well influence the eventual direction taken; developments which have undoubtedly benefited from the growth during the 1970s and 1980s of single-employer bargaining.(10) Trade unions, instead of leading on the issue, could well be dragged into policy making in response to new patterns of working time. If this is the case, the possibility of a coherent unified approach would seem to be as remote in the future as it has been in the past.

Bargaining working time

Despite (or, perhaps, because of) the vacuum at the top and the lack of any clear trade-union policy initiatives on working time, company and plant-wide bargaining has produced a heterogeneous mixture of practices. Innovations have taken place, but they have often been at the behest of the employer or, on occasion, of the employees. Management have dictated the agenda whilst the shop-floor have sought to bargain and exercise a degree of control over the details.(11) The trade union impetus to change has been slight and, as a consequence, the unions have often either been bypassed in the change process or, at best, had to endorse practices with which they disagree (particularly in the area of shift working).(12) The result has been that, rather than spearheading change, the unions have been seen to be dragging their feet on the issue. A number of areas illustrate the point.

Overtime

Trade unions have been reluctant, or unable, to link reductions in the working week with the restriction or removal of systematic overtime working. The TUC has argued the case, but collective bargaining has proved a poor regulatory mechanism.(13) This has provided employers with a powerful argument against reduced working time (14) and employees with little incentive to seek radical cuts in hours, though there is some evidence that about half Britain's working population would opt for shorter hours for the same pay as opposed to better pay for the same hours.(15) Trade unions are often the 'managers' or 'regulators' of overtime rather than the proponents of shorter working time and overtime elimination.(16) There is more overtime worked per overtime worker now with unemployment at well over two million than there was five years ago when unemployment was 'only' 1.3 million. Chapter 6 examines the question of overtime in greater depth.

Shift working

Trade unions have viewed shift working with deep suspicion and have often opposed night working. However, shift working is here to stay and it could provide opportunities to reduce both the working week and, more importantly, annual working time, particularly when five-crew shift working is involved. Employees have often initiated and adopted shift working practices to this effect.(17)

However, the British trade union movement is reluctant to recognize it as a vehicle for progress and has not made, for example, five-crew shift working (in the case of continuous production) a major bargaining issue - unlike many of its European counterparts (including the ETUC and the European Metalworkers' Federation). It has reached the paradoxical situation where four-crew systems, producing 1,800 plus individual contractual hours per year and a further 100 hours overtime built into the system, are approved - even recommended - and yet 12-hour systems, producing 1,600-1,700 annual hours and little or no overtime, are frowned upon.(18) Employees have often voted with their feet for longer shift/longer leisure block systems with a consequent shift in the levers of shop-floor bargaining.(19) (See Chapters 7 and 8 for further discussion of shiftwork innovations).

The 'manual' - 'staff' divide

Harmonization between the working hours of blue-collar and white-collar workers in Britain has been slow to take off, although recent evidence points to greater movement in this area.(20) Part of the problem lies with the fragmentation of the British trade union movement (as well as Britain's 'class' and 'status' system which it, in part, mirrors). White-collar unions (ASTMS - now MSF - being a good example) have recruited on the basis of the preferential terms and conditions they could negotiate for their members. When allied to an existing system which has traditionally meant that manual workers work longer hours than their non-manual colleagues (the opposite is often the case on the Continent) (21), differentials in working time have developed. Even where holidays have been harmonized, weekly hours have often remained untouched.(22) As a means of bargaining reduced working time, 'harmonization' is a powerful weapon. At shop-floor level, it is one which is beginning to be employed. At national level advocacy is often muted, even where apparent, as Britain's large general unions which dominate the TUC (the TGWU, AEU, GMB and EETPU) often contain white-collar sections and a 'mixed' membership.(23)

New working patterns

It is fairly easy to be critical of the trade union movement's approach to reorganized working time.(24) At best it has been a series of good intentions with few suggestions as to how theory can be translated into practice e.g. TUC 1984.(25) Equally, in the case of labour flexibility, the union response has been highly fragmented with wide disparities between national policies and local agreements. However, these problems have as much to do with union structures as with union attitudes. Union autonomy has mitigated against any coherent approach beyond the bland and the mundane and what we have seen is a whole range of different approaches by different unions (often different approaches by the same union) to suit particular contingencies or circumstances. Some of these can be seen as progressive, others less so.

Trade unions have generally found new working patterns to be a threat and a reflex negativity has characterized official responses. The opportunities of greater personal choice over working time and some of the benefits of greater personal flexibility have been either down-played or over-looked. Meanwhile at plant level workers have been voting with their feet. As Atkinson and Gregory correctly observed in regard to union responses to flexibility initiatives:

> There is a clear gap emerging between the rhetoric of resistance and the reality at the place of work.(26)

Flexibility is fashionable - the managerial buzz-word of the 1980s. However, it would be wrong to conclude because it was fashionable that it was likely to be a short-lived phenomenon. The evidence suggests otherwise. Movement towards greater occupational and workforce flexibility will continue apace in most sectors of the economy. In some areas the change will be fairly marginal (a bit more sub-contracting, a few more 'temps'), in others it will be radical (e.g. the increasing use of part timers in retail and distribution, flexible craftsmen and the extension of shiftwork). Trade unions will be forced to adjust their thinking and the extent to which they do so will largely determine their influence over change. Most major unions, whatever the rhetoric at the top, have shown themselves capable of at least thinking of making the necessary adjustments. However, to what extent this might prove adequate in terms of future labour market developments is more open to question.

<u>Flexi-time</u>

The operation of flexi-time on a core-hours system has been almost exclusively a phenomenon of white-collar, office workers.(27) The office worker has sought greater freedom by going on-the-clock whilst its blue-collar counterpart has been trying to get off it. White collar trade unions appear to be broadly sympathetic to flexi-time systems, even though it breaches notions of the 8-hour day.(28) The lack of historical interest in the 8-hour day among white collar unions may explain this collective flexibility. For the railway workers when faced with 'flexible rostering', the perceived breach of an historical union milestone proved one of the main obstacles to agreement.(29) Further union criticisms concerning the payment of overtime have also been expressed. Nevertheless, employees appear to favour it, particularly women workers. Employers also have been supportive, although again predominantly within a white-collar context.

The development of flexi-time systems to embrace the flexi-year, e.g. by <u>annual time contracts</u> remains in its infancy; although here there appears to be much wider scope for development in blue-collar areas.(30) Forms of annual time contracts have been pioneered in the refinery industries. The main difference between flexi-year and flexi-time system lies in the degree of discretion over holidays and leisure blocks - ideally a flexi-year system should allow greater discretion. Again trade union stances have been conservative - flexi-year systems may well involve longer shifts (10 or 12 hours) and periodically longer working weeks. The fact that annual working time contracts may limit or remove overtime tends to be ignored by a movement which finds it hard to think in terms other than a weekly wage for a defined working week on the basis of an 8-hour day. (See Chapter 8 for further analysis of flexi-time issues).

Part time work

For trade unions heavily reliant on full time male workers the growth of female part time employment has been bad news.(31) It would have been worse news were it not for the narrow occupational classification of the bulk of part timers within primarily two categories of service sector work (food, retail and distribution and 'others'). Under protective legislation trade unions expanded their membership in the 1970s despite making hardly any inroads regarding the unionization of part time workers. The 1980s have proved a much harsher climate for union recruitment and they have lost nearly a quarter of total membership. The reality of this situation has forced unions to take a closer look at attitudes to part time work.(32) A catastrophic decline in manufacturing has to be weighed against the fact that part time employment accounted for two-thirds of the growth in the service sector during the 1970s(33) - it is unlikely to be less in the 1980s. If the service sector is to take up the employment slack in the economy, it is more likely to do it on the basis of part time jobs than full time jobs. Trade unions have to face up to this fact. Employer preference for part timers is likely to increase as the occupational spread of part time work increases. (See Chapter 7 for further discussion of part time working).

For the trade union movement the employment shift to the service sector and the growth of part time employment in that sector represents a profound challenge. Outside of the public sector, there is little evidence that that challenge is being effectively met. It is not necessary to fully subscribe to the 'flexible firm' thesis of 'core' and 'peripheral' workers (34), to appreciate the reality of the situation and the fact that in many cases the spread of 'non-permanent' workers is being tolerated in order to strengthen the job security of full timers. The weakness of union bargaining positions in the recession (seldom conceded by either trade union leaders or their critics) has been exploited to insert various categories of 'non-employees' into the main workforce e.g. youth trainees, part timers, self-employed, sub-contractors, and temporary or casual workers. The spread of temporary work has perhaps the gravest implications for the trade union movement.

Temporary work

In April 1983, 19.2 per cent of Jobcentre vacancies filled were for temporary work - by January 1985 this had almost doubled to 38.2 per cent. In areas of high unemployment temporary work is often the only work available; although financially unavailable to married men with dependent children.

Other aspects of the growth of temporary work ought to cause alarm-bells to ring for the trade union movement. The spread of temporary work cannot be viewed in the same light as part time work. Temporary workers are more likely to be women but not on anything like the scale of part timers. A recent large-scale survey found in a sample where just under 50 per cent of employees were female, some one-third of all temporary workers were male. Further, use of temporary workers was concentrated among the larger and faster growing organizations. The scale of temporary work in the sample was 8 per cent of total employees and some use of temporary work in 75 per cent of organizations surveyed.(35) It has been suggested that the 'temp' of the future is as likely to be male as female, and often professional rather than secretarial. Equally, there is plenty of case study evidence to point to the growth of temporary work in mainstream manufacturing, where the motivation has often been the post-1979 redundancy experience rather than the more traditional need for temporary cover through illness, holidays or seasonal demand.

The data regarding temporary work remains patchy and should be treated with some caution. Nevertheless, it is accumulating and does suggest an expansion in white-collar areas (36) and in manufacturing and public utilities. Where temporary workers are used, the evidence does not indicate appreciably worse terms and conditions of employment but their status is more questionable. One recent agreement at a unionized plant stated five conditions for the employment of temporary workers. Point 5 reads:

> Temporary employees have no voting rights on decisions affecting wages and conditions of employment of permanent employees.

This is, in essence, a form of occupational apartheid. The terms and conditions of permanent employees establish those for temporary employees. It precludes 'temps' from having any in-put into settlements which directly affect them. They provide a job security buffer to the permanent workforce with little or no employment rights. As it is assumed that their status makes them less likely to take industrial action or be union-conscious, it appears to be in the vested interests of the unions to deny them equal rights (they become similar to the German 'guest-workers').

The growth of part time employment has been largely restricted to a number of areas within the service sector. This would not appear to be the case with temporary work. Of course, under current employment law, employers may regard all employees with less than two years service as temporary (unless they happen to be anti-union, black or pregnant). However, few choose to fully exploit the government's legal libertarianism. The use of temporary workers is a more insidious threat to employment conditions as it paradoxically strengthens the position of 'permanents' (many of whom may have less than two years service), whilst providing permanent insecurity and few rights to the minority.

Trade union strategies to cope with the utilization of temporary workers are, as yet, noticeable by their absence. Saying that it is a product of mass unemployment and changes in the labour market does not make it go away. It is likely to become institutionalized, possibly as widely in the public sector as the private, and brings closer to reality the concepts of the 'flexible firm' and 'flexible organization'.

Job sharing

Outside of a few cases which can be best viewed as part time work rather than job sharing, the growth of job sharing has been the almost exclusive preserve of professional women in public sector employment.(37) As far as the trade union movement is concerned involvement has been limited to those unions where a degree of membership interest has been aroused e.g. NALGO. It is difficult to envisage a rapid expansion of job sharing in its true sense or, for that matter, 'job-splitting' in the peculiar sense in which the government appears to conceive it. Few employers are likely to opt for job sharing in preference to part time work and few trade unions seem anxious to promote the concept. The positive contribution which job sharing could make to the employment conditions of those on reduced hours is likely to be of benefit to only a fortunate few. The more job sharing continues to be perceived as a luxury for middle-class, professional women, the more likely it is that other forms of voluntary reduced time will be seen in a similar light. Individual choice over working time will continue to be restricted until one or more large employer pioneer innovations and one or more large trade unions outside of white-collar work take a practical (as opposed to a theoretical) interest in the subject.(38)

The 'flexible-firm' debate and trade unions

It is clear that definite trends towards greater labour flexibility can be discerned. What can be questioned is their scale and cohesion. The majority of the working population do not work part time; temporary work could be viewed as still a relatively minor and possibly transient sector of the labour market; and interest in job sharing remains extremely modest. Is it a fuss about not very much - a problem which the trade union movement can safely ignore or treat as a minor irritant? It is argued here that to see it in such terms - a not over-simplified or over-exaggerated characterization of the contemporary trade union response - is to badly underestimate the structural changes in operation. The issues which lie at the heart of the flexibility debate - employment conditions, personal choice, improved training and greater job autonomy - are central to the trade union movement and to its future.

To begin to understand the importance of these issues, it is perhaps first of all necessary to discard the academic ideal-type of 'flexible firm'. It may be a good analytical tool but it is less useful for union bargainers who may never meet such an animal. What they are likely to meet is a variety of firms who are adapting in different ways to different aspects of the so-called 'flexible firm'. One company may wish to make small sections of its workforce self-employed; another might want to extend its use of sub-contractors; another might want to have more 'temps' in the office; another might wish to make its maintenance workforce more flexible; another would like to take advantage of cheap youth trainees; another might be seeking an agreement on the use of casual workers to meet seasonal or market fluctuations; etc., etc. The reality is more likely to be this kind of series of 'one-off', ad hoc measures rather than a strategic blueprint to transform the nature of a company's work organization or working conditions. This is not to deny that in certain companies, particularly large transnational organizations, there may well be an overall strategy to progress towards something approaching the 'flexible firm'. It is merely to state that at least nine times out of ten work reorganization is likely to take the form of a single particular development which will probably have nothing to do with the immediate establishment of a dual labour force. Piecemeal and company-specific developments will far outweigh the 'ideal-types'.

Thus, for trade union negotiators, the view that any move in any of these directions is the 'thin-end-of-the-wedge' and therefore to be opposed is unlikely to be mirrored on the shop-floor. To claim that flexibility is wrong and is to be resisted, fails to take into account the potential advantages which particular forms of flexibility have for particular groups of workers. Just as company approaches are likely to be pragmatic, so will the trade union movement need to be pragmatic in its responses if it is to carry its members with it. The trade union approach needs to be selective, even 'opportunistic'. To resist flexibility is to deny that such opportunities exist. If negotiators at national level do not perceive the prospect of positive rewards, those at local plant level almost certainly will and will make arrangements accordingly. The less the trade union movement is associated with real gains and benefits in employment conditions, the weaker their representational function becomes. As companies increasingly look towards establishing a more 'company union' perspective, the dangers to strong independent trade unionism become apparent. As well as retaining influence over existing members there is also the problem of recruiting new members - particularly in high technology industries and the service sector where anti-unionism is strong and traditional organization weak.

All is not doom and gloom for the trade union movement. However, it would be foolish to pretend that trade unions in Britain had established an image of positive and pragmatic behaviour where reduced working time and labour flexibility was concerned. In the current political climate of privatization, de-regulation and the weakening of statutory provisions, a defensive reaction is perhaps understandable. Nevertheless, the underlying changes in the labour market owe little to any of these forces and <u>will</u> long outlast them. To believe otherwise is delusive.

Working time developments: what price change?

Collective bargaining revolves around proposals, negotiations, offers and agreements. Trade unions and employees may not exercise a great deal of control over the latter two items, but they can set the bargaining agenda. Part of the argument of this chapter has been that trade unions have stuck rigidly to the pursuit of the shorter working week to the exclusion of other, perhaps more viable, options in regard to shorter working time. However, there are, it is argued, a number of indications which all the bargaining agencies - but particularly trade unions - would be foolish to ignore:(39)

The EEC has developed a draft recommendation on working time (40) - a policy proposal to which the strongest opposition has come from the UK Government. In it, the EEC postulated a reduction in individual annual working time of 10 per cent over a fixed time span. It proposed more flexible forms of work organization, productivity increases to contribute to job creation rather than wages, incentives for geographical occupational mobility, the removal of obstacles to workforce expansion (particularly tax and insurance inhibitions), the restriction of systematic overtime and the rewarding of overtime by time off in lieu, and support for changes in the pattern of working life cycles to encourage individual work/leisure trade-offs (the draft directive on part time work and strengthened employee rights being seen as particularly important in this area).(41) It is too early to say how much influence the EEC will be able to exert in these areas, although prospective majority voting may help. However, it is an agenda which the British trade union movement has barely begun to address and yet one which, if implemented, would have profound effects on bargaining.

The employers (notably the CBI) have taken a tough position on working time. However, there are signs - and the recent position of the engineering employers is just one - that employers are willing to bargain reductions in and reorganization of working time for greater workforce flexibility.(42) The introduction of new technology has been a powerful catalyst in the process, though the trade unions' response to it has had only limited success.(43) The bargains which are struck, and the way in which productivity gains are rewarded, will have an immense bearing on future working patterns and working life cycles. The onus and the options in these areas are not the sole prerogative of management, but trade unions have shown a marked reluctance to promote productivity/working time trade-offs aggressively, partly because they have felt excluded from the process of technological change and partly because they have feared that working time reductions may involve income reductions. Government has largely eschewed responsibility for intervention in the labour market. It has opposed shorter working time as a means of job creation.(44) However, it is having to face the public expenditure burden of mass unemployment, the extension of youth training and an expanding number of state pensioners. There are few signs that is is prepared to take major initiatives in regard to working time ('job release' being a partial success and 'job splitting' a disaster). However, it has proved amenable to schemes which remove people from being recipients of unemployment benefit. The bargaining options in this area appear extremely narrow, but none the less might prove particularly relevant.

Individual attitudes towards working time could well be the most influential factor in the whole process whilst, at the same time, proving the most difficult to assess. Surveys consistently show that people want more leisure time and place considerable value on it - though the degree to which they are prepared to trade leisure for income remains problematic.(45) At workplace level, however, there is evidence that - given the choice - people will opt to maximize leisure blocks and minimize annual working time. In the working time debate, particularly where technological change is involved, such attitudes could be of great significance in determining future patterns of work.

In all four areas, there are signs that collective bargaining agencies will come under increasing pressure with regard to reducing individual working time. However, that is not to say that such signs are necessarily being correctly interpreted or understood. An examination of a number of key developments will bear out such uncertainties.

Trends in reduced working time

Five trends in the area of reduced working time can be discerned which have important implications for bargainers:

1 <u>Life cycles</u> The working lifetime of male workers has been reduced by 10 per cent during the 70s (approximately 100,000 to 90,000 hours) and will probably be reduced by a similiar proportion during the 80s.(46) This has very little or nothing to do with the shorter working week (which has only fallen from 40 to 39.1 in that time) - the cornerstone of trade union demands - but is primarily a consequence of later entry into the labour market and earlier withdrawal from it. The main factors at work here are the external forces of demanning and state regulation. Bargaining, particularly in areas of flexible and phased retirement, could influence this trend, but it is more likely to be reactive - dealing/coping with nationalization - than proactive.

2 <u>New working patterns</u> The movement towards contracting out of chunks of work by major companies and organizations (mainly at the lower end, but also including 'networking' for managers), the development of 'home working' and the growth of part time work, will all contrive to make more complex working time arrangements.(47) Quite separate conditions of employment and negotiations may develop between the 'core' and 'peripheral' workforces. A 'core' workforce, operating on a 35-hour week, could be underpinned by groups of contractors, part timers, home workers, operating on different, perhaps even longer, hours. The 'core' could be unionized, but the 'peripheral' may not. Trade unions have yet to think through the implications of these changes.(48)

3 <u>New technology</u> The spread of information technology has provided opportunities for trade unions and bargainers to negotiate reduced working time. However, this has not always been (perhaps seldom) job creative, and major working-time changes have often been the consequence of new forms of work organization, e.g. the much-heralded 32½-hour week for technicians at Westland Helicopters was negotiated on the basis of an acceptance of CAD/CAM and a movement from day work to shift work. New technology bargaining has powerful implications with regard to demarcation, differentials and more flexible working practices. It is seldom a straight trade-off between technology/productivity and jobs/working time.

4 <u>Harmonization</u> The attempt to remove differentials between white-collar workers' contractual hours and those of blue-collar workers has led to working time reductions. This will no doubt continue to be a bargaining issue, but having 'caught up', both sections of the workforce might find the prospect of further reductions hampered by the need for an across-the-board settlement - just as industry-wide bargainers have had greater difficulty in negotiating working time reductions than those operating at a company/organization or plant-wide basis. Existing data point to a 'harmonization' trend but not a 'convergence' (such as on the 35-hour week) trend.

5 Shift-work innovations   As a consequence of new technology and more sophisticated machinery, employers are eager to utilize their equipment on a longer basis than nine to five for five days a week. Manufacturing has had a long experience of semi-continuous and continuous production systems. Now white-collar areas are witnessing such developments as computer technology, it assumes greater importance. Equally, there is a discernible move to longer hours in many of the service industries, and the development of 24-hour servicing in some. Where new technology is involved, the opportunity to bargain shorter hours exists, and has been taken in many well publicized instances. In manufacturing, five-crew shift working is on the increase. There is also a trend towards 12-hour shift working, which again has a range of implications for the bargaining of reduced working time. Innovations in shift-working patterns and flexible work schedules will undoubtedly continue to provide the standard-bearers of the reduced working time movement, but concessions will only be gained at a cost to traditional working practices and patterns of work.

The five trends delineated above have one thing in common. None is a consequence of an attempt to cope with the social misery of mass unemployment. They all potentially point in the direction of reduced working time, but not through any conscious attempt at work redistribution. This has certain implications for trade unions in particular and bargaining in general. The conclusions of this chapter are devoted to an appraisal of those implications.

Conclusions

This chapter has sought to argue a number of points:

1 the lack of a coherent trade union strategy for reducing working time beyond extolling the virtues of a 35-hour week and the need for early retirement;

2 the clear inability of trade unions to control individual annual working time through a failure to tackle overtime and endorse policies which might minimize it;

3 innovations in, and control over, working time have largely rested with management and to a lesser degree employees - trade unions have fought a rearguard, rather than an offensive, action;

4 there are pressures - from the EEC, employers, government and employees - which could significantly affect the bargaining of reduced working time, but most imply some kind of trade-off between hours and productivity or hours and income;

5 the major developments in reduced working time which can be discerned are primarily as a consequence of rationalization and new technology - new working patterns are emerging (often associated with shorter working hours), but not through any desire to create jobs, to redistribute work or to ameliorate the lot of the unemployed.

If the above analysis is broadly accurate, trade unions (or employee representatives) will be most effective in reducing hours where some kind of trade-off or bargain between hours/income/productivity/technology/work organization is struck. All the major breakthroughs on hours in the last six years conform to this pattern. This may appear to be self evident. However, it is not accepted as such by either the trade union movement as a whole, employers or by government.

Trade unions argue the case for a shorter working week as a matter of social policy and have chosen to ignore both the factors and innovations which have effectively reduced working time in the past and hold out the best prospects in the future. Employers have adopted the stance that all working time reductions automatically raise unit costs and that any form of work redistribution suffers from the 'lump of labour fallacy'. They have made innovations to work organization and new patterns of working time, but seldom as a consequence of bargains struck to reduce individual annual working time or to create jobs.

Government has viewed working hours reductions as another symptom of the all-pervading disease of employees pricing themselves out of jobs. There has been no recognition that people working long hours are working others out of jobs, or that many of our major competitors have shorter working hours and tighter controls over working time. The encouragement of productivity bargaining to create jobs through shorter working time has been minimal (whilst 3.5 million-plus are being paid to do no work at all).

The conclusion drawn is that the bargaining of reduced working time, let alone of work sharing, is still in its infancy. Developments are piecemeal and ad hoc, and bear no relation to any employment strategy for job creation. The opportunities which exist for widening job opportunities by means of new patterns of working time are not being grasped because of a conservatism of approach which affects all sides of the bargaining table.

In the past, working time has been reduced and standards of living raised as a direct consequence of productivity increases. We do not work the same hours as our Victorian forebears, nor under the same conditions, nor for the same wages, and there is no good reason why we ever should. The causal link between technological development and greater leisure has to be firmly accepted, and workplace bargains struck on that basis. However, to do so, trade unions will need to look beyond an hour or two off the 'normal' working week and early retirement.

Past performance does not give a great deal of cause for optimism. Trade unions would be better advised to adopt a more pragmatic approach on hours at workplace level rather than, as at present, putting ever finer detail on a blueprint for some future Labour Government. Trade union bargaining in the past was not based on a Joe Hill - 'you'll get pie in the sky when you die' - approach. Although the collective bargaining of reduced working time will be severely constrained vis-a-vis its job creation potential, the price to be paid for a failure to tackle the problem adequately could well prove high - particularly for trade unions.

Trade unions are struggling to cope with technological and labour market changes. To summarize in regard to working time, the TUC does not have a comprehensible policy on overtime, neither does it have a clear-cut strategy in any of the major areas of innovation in working time in recent years i.e. part time work, annual time contracts, flexi-time, five-crew shiftworking, longer leisure blocks and job sharing. Emphasis is placed on the shorter working week and earlier retirement as these appear to be the two areas on which common agreement prevails. Elsewhere, in the absence of policy, unions are left to their own devices to cobble together some approach or not as the case may be. Invariably the approach is defensive and piecemeal. Meanwhile membership is slipping away and the world of work is moving on.

Notes

1. The TUC's policies have been outlined in successive annual economic reviews and their pursuit in the General Council's annual reports to Congress. See particularly, 'The Battle for Jobs', <u>TUC Economic Review</u>, TUC, London, 1983, and TUC-Labour Party Liaison Committee - '<u>Economic Planning and Industrial Democracy: The Framework for Full Employment</u>', Report to the 1982 TUC Congress and Labour Party Conference, Labour Party, London, 1982.
2. The TUC launched its Campaign for Reduced Working Time in 1979 as part of a European-wide movement, but it is only recently that notions of work sharing or work redistribution have been seriously considered. The TUC has published a series of 'Progress Reports' (Nos. 1-12) covering changes in hours and working time as part of the campaign.
3. The 35-hour week is equally the main plank of the European Trade Union Confederation (ETUC) proposals regarding working time, but it has gone further than the TUC in arguing for a fifth shift for round-the-clock shift work and payment for excessive overtime to be in time off in lieu; see, European Trade Union Institute, '<u>Working Time in Western Europe in 1982</u>', European Trade Union Institute, Brussels, 1983.
4. For a survey of European practice vis-a-vis working time, see European Trade Union Institute, 'Working Time in Western Europe in 1982', <u>ibid</u>. and European Trade Union Institute, '<u>Practical Experiences with the Reduction of Working Time in Europe</u>', European Trade Union Institute, Brussels, 1984.
5. The December 1984 figures, for average weekly overtime per worker and actual hours of overtime worked in manufacturing industry, were the highest for five years. Equally, the average hours of full time manual workers in 1984 were higher than the comparable figures for 1982 and 1983. See 'Earnings and Hours of Manual Employees in 1984', <u>Employment Gazette</u>, February 1985, p.49.
6. The CBI recently claimed to have 'stopped the rot on hours' - 'CBI Slams Shorter Week', <u>The Sunday Times</u>, 18 September 1983, p.59.
7. The TUC's latest 'Working time action check-list for negotiators' did endorse job sharing for the first time and strongly pressed for tighter controls on overtime. See 'New TUC Guidelines on Reducing Working Time', <u>Industrial Relations Review and Report</u>, No. 330, 23 October 1984, pp. 11-12.
8. No specific figure in regard to annual permissible overtime hours has been formulated.
9. See, for example, TUC Campaign for Reduced Working Time - '<u>Progress Report</u>', No. 9, 1983.
10. See Brown, W. (Ed.), <u>The Changing Contours of British Industrial Relations</u>, Basil Blackwell, Oxford, 1981 and Deaton, D. and Beaumont, P., 'The Determinants of Bargaining Structure. Some Large Scale Survey Evidence'. <u>British Journal of Industrial Relations</u>, Vol. 18 No. 2, July 1980.
11. For a discussion of this issue within the context of a specific case study - the introduction of 'flexible rostering' on British

Rail – see Lee, R., 'Hours of Work – Who Controls and How', *Industrial Relations Journal*, Vol. 14 No. 4, Winter 1983, pp. 70-5; for a wider discussion of the question see Smith, R., 'The Maximization of Control in Industrial Relations', in Purcell, J. and Smith, R. (Eds.), *The Control of Work*, MacMillan, London, 1979, pp. 1-26.

12. The author knows of no national trade union which endorses 12-hour shift working and yet it is undoubtedly on the increase – often arising out of employee demand in certain instances, e.g. the move to five-crew shift working at American Can (Runcorn), the company and the unions have resisted employee pressure to operate a 12-hour system; but where companies have provided choice in regard to new shift-working arrangements, e.g. the introduction of a five-crew system at Esso Fawley, trade union opposition to 12-hour working has been unable to carry the day.

13. A weakness exhibited across a range of work-sharing measures; see Plyton, P., 'The Industrial Relations of Work Sharing', *Industrial Relations Journal*, Vol. 3 No. 3, Autumn 1982, pp. 6-12; Hart, R. A., *Shorter Working Time – A Dilemma for Collective Bargaining*, OECD, Paris, 1984.

14. Well-voiced in the CBI's discussion document, '*Jobs – Facing the Future*', CBI, London, January 1980, pp. 37-47; the overtime spin-off has been a major plank of the present Government's opposition to the EEC Directive on working time.

15. See Jones, S.G., 'The Work-sharing Debate in Western Europe', *Quarterly Review, National Westminster Bank*, February 1985.

16. A case I have argued at greater length elsewhere, see Paul Rathkey, 'Work and the Prisoners of Time – The Case for Work Sharing', *op. cit.*

17. See for example, McEwan Young, W., 'Shiftwork and Flexible Schedules: Are they Compatible?', *International Labour Review*, Vol. 119 No. 1, January/February 1980, pp. 1-17.

18. There may well be sound health reasons for opposing 12-hour shifts, but this argument ought equally to be applied where excessive overtime operates. The debate ought equally to be applied where excessive overtime operates. The debate on shift working and health is clouded by a lack of adequate data. For an excellent 'state-of-the-art' review, see Harrington, J.M., '*Shift Work and Health, A Critical Review of the Literature*', HMSO, London 1978.

19. See, for example, 'Shiftwork 2, Reducing Working Hours', *Industrial Relations Review and Report*, No. 308, 22 November 1983, pp. 2-7.

20. See, for example, 'Hours and Holidays', *Incomes Data Services Study*, No. 300, October 1983.

21. See Euro-fiet, *Employment Creation and Working Time*, Brussels, 1983, p. 43.

22. It is said that harmonized holidays now exist in over 50 per cent of companies (see, 'Holiday Entitlement' 2: Company Provision,' *Industrial Relations Review and Report* No. 327, 11 September 1984, pp. 2-10), however, there has been strong white-collar union opposition to harmonized hours – see IDS Study No. 300, *op. cit.*

23. For example, the Confederation of Shipbuilding and Engineering Unions (CSEU) has accepted a policy that the working hours of white-collar workers should not stand still whilst those of their blue-collar colleagues catch up, see IDS Study No. 300, *op. cit.*, p.4.

24. See P. Rathkey – 'British trade unions rethink work time', *Work Times* Vol. 2 No. 4, July 1984, pp. 1-4.

25. TUC - <u>Working time: objectives and guidelines for trade union negotations</u> (London, 1984).
26. J. Atkinson and D. Gregory - 'A flexible future: Britain's dual labour force', <u>Marxism Today</u>, Vol. 30 No. 4, April 1986, pp. 12-17.
27. See, for example, IDS - <u>Flexible working hours</u> (Incomes Data Services Study No. 301, November, 1983).
28. See R. Lee - 'Trade union attitudes to flexible working hours', <u>Industrial Relations Journal</u> Vol. 14 No. 1, Spring 1983, pp. 80-83.
29. See P. Rathkey - <u>The Challenge of Change: A study of technology and industrial relations on British Rail</u> (Jim Conway Foundation, Stockton, November 1986).
30. See B. Teriet - 'Flexiyear Schedules - only a matter of time?', <u>Monthly Labour Review</u>, Washington D.C., December 1977, pp. 62-5.
31. For a discussion of this growth see O. Robinson - The changing labour market: the phenomena of part time employment in Britain', <u>National Westminster Bank Quarterly Review</u>, November 1985, pp. 19-29.
32. See, for example, IRRR - 'Part time work: a survey' <u>Industrial Relations Review and Reports</u>, No. 320, May 1984, pp. 2-9.
33. G. Clark - 'Recent developments in working patterns' <u>Employment Gazette</u> July 1982, pp. 284-88.
34. See, for example, J. Atkinson - <u>Manning for uncertainty - some emerging UK work patterns</u> (Institute of Manpower Studies, Sussex University, 1984).
35. N. Meager - 'Temporary work in Britain' <u>Employment Gazette</u>, January 1986, pp. 7-15.
36. M. Syrett - <u>Temporary work today</u> (Federation of Recruitment and Employment Services, London, 1985).
37. See particularly, the Equal Opportunties Commission report on 'Job Sharing, op. cit; Boyle, A., '<u>Job Sharing: A Study of the Costs, Benefits and Employment Rights of Job Sharers</u>', New Ways to Work, London, 1980; Clutterbuck, D. and Hill, R., The Remaking of Work, op. cit., pp., 59-69.
38. A reluctance not just peculiar to British trade unions. See Benson, J., 'Trade Union Attitudes to Job Sharing in Australia and Some Lessons for the UK', <u>Industrial Relations Journal</u>, Autumn 1982, Vol. 13, No. 3, pp. 13-9.
39. This report is particularly concerned with the problems of work distribution within the 'core' period of working life cycles; it does not cover devices for delaying entry into the labour market (e.g. youth training schemes) or for encouraging withdrawal from it (e.g. flexible, phased, or early retirement).
40. See European Commission - '<u>Draft Recommendation on the Reduction and Reorganization of Working Time</u>', EEC, Brussels, December 1982, pp. 12-4.
41. See European Commission - '<u>Memorandum on the Reduction and Reorganization of Working Time</u>', COM(82) 809 final, EEC, Brussels, December 1982, pp. 12-4.
42. See, for example, 'Shorter Working Week: An IR-RR Review' <u>Industrial Relations Review and Report</u> No. 312, 24 January 1984, pp. 2-7; 'Hours and Holidays 1984', <u>Incomes Data Services Study</u>, No. 323, October 1984.
43. For details of that response see Robins, K. and Webster, F. 'New Technoloogy: A Survey of Trade Union Reponse in Britain', <u>Industrial Relations Journal</u>, Vol 13 No. 1, Spring 1982, pp. 7-26; Manwaring, T., 'The Trade Union Response to New Technology',

44. <u>Industrial Relations Journal</u>, Vol. 12 No. 4, July-August 1981, pp. 7-26; Bamber, G. and Willman, P., 'Technological Change and Industrial Relations in Britain', <u>Bulletin of Comparative Labour Relations</u>, Vol. 12, Summer 1983.
45. The initial reasoning can be traced to the Department of Employment paper, 'Measures to Alleviate Unemployment in the Medium Term: Work Sharing', <u>Employment Gazette</u>, Vol. 86, No. 4, April 1978, pp. 400-2. However, unemployment has trebled since then without any shift in policy.
46. Recent Scandinavian governmental studies have shown support for taking shorter hours rather than higher wages (incomes remaining constant) but little support (below 20 per cent) for time-income trade-offs, See Grohn, K. '<u>Views on Shortening Daily Working Hours</u>', Ministry of Social Affairs and Health Research, Department Paper No. 15, Juikaisoja Publications, Helsinki, October 1979, and Committee for the Study of Working Hours (DELFA), '<u>Preferred Working Hours</u>', Ministry of Labour, Stockholm, 1984.
46. Armstrong, P. '<u>Technical Change and Reductions in Life Hours of Work</u>', Technical Change Centre, London, 1984, p. 27.
47. See, Atkinson, J., '<u>New Patterns of Working Relationships</u>', Institute of Manpower Studies, Sussex University, 1984; <u>Managing News Patterns of Work</u>, British Institute of Management, Corby, 1985.
48. See Rathkey, P. 'British Trade Unions and New Patterns of Working Time', <u>Work Times</u>, Vol. 2 No. 4, July 1984, pp. 1-4.

4 Case studies of work re-organization and time innovations

Introduction

The case study element of the project sought to examine some of the major innovations in the reorganization of operational time currently taking place at plant level within the United Kingdom. With reference to the key areas highlighted in Chapter 1, the cases chosen reflected many of the major developments:

Life-cycles (shorter working time) - Cases 1-4
Flexible patterns - Cases 1-4
Part time working - Case 2
New technology (primarily) - Case 1
Harmonization - Case 3
Shiftwork innovations - Cases 1,3 and 4

The case studies are, of course, illustrative rather than representative and their focus was based on an examination of a number of key areas:

1 the process of change/innovation/reorganization
2 new working patterns
3 manpower utilization - level and structure
4 employment implications
5 productivity/efficiency gains
6 working conditions and trade-offs (income-time-rewards)
7 industrial relations consequences.

Methodology

Case study selection was based on the nature of the change involved. Approaches were made to ten companies in all where a major reorganization of operational time had recently occurred, i.e. one which fell within one or more of the major areas of innovation previously defined. The research project was limited to four case studies and the desire to include the railway study - a partial examination but a major reorganization of wide significance - left the project requiring a further three plant-level studies. Within the limited time available for the research, it did not prove possible to follow up the prospect of case studies with all the companies initially approached. Following the initial invitations to participate in the project, four companies expressed an interest. Agreement with three companies providing a balanced range of studies - a major shiftwork innovation, a development of part time working and a large harmonization exercise - was concluded and these are the studies whose main findings are summarized in this chapter (other case study evidence both by the author and other researchers is cited elsewhere in this report in support of the potential impact of the trends under discussion).

In making the approaches and selection a number of points need to be stressed. The research timetable was very tight and companies who had just gone through an exercise in work reorganization were felt likely to be sensitive to exposure to outside bodies. At least, it was assumed from past experience (the JCF has conducted other case studies at plant-level into new patterns of working time) to be the case. Therefore, almost by definition, the companies who agreed to participate believed that their reorganization exercises had been successful. In two instances where companies approached did not express an interest, it was known to the researchers that difficulties were being experienced with the new system (one with a 'harmonization' scheme and another with a 5-crew shiftworking scheme among a very large - 6000 - workforce). Participation in the project was voluntary and in all research studies of this kind, a degree of self-selection has to be added to the external selection made by the researchers. The case studies, therefore, are more illustrative of successful work reorganizations than those with major difficulties (though in fact this was not true of the railways study - Case Study 4).

Another point concerning selection was the strong emphasis which the researchers placed on company confidentiality. From past experience, this has proved to be the major stumbling block to access (as the research team operates out of a largely trade union-based organization this is perhaps not surprising). The research timetable was short - six months from initial approaches to report completion - and to obtain company co-operation, anonymity and information confidentiality were seen as essential factors.

The case studies therefore concentrated on the nature of the work reorganization and excluded much company background material. A further possible weakness was the lack of detailed statistical information regarding the costs of reorganization and the impact on productivity. Where detailed information was available - in two companies - it was regarded as 'sensitive' and was not included in the final published reports. However, accepting these limitations, it has to be stated that the four companies co-operated very fully with the research and accepted it as an independent examination.

The methodology employed was a standard semi-structured interview schedule approach to a cross-section of staff - managers, supervisors, trade union representatives and employees - directly involved with the work reorganization itself. In most cases these were supplemented by a range of quantitative information - agreements, shift-cycles, etc. In two of the studies, access to the minutes of working parties and company reports proved of considerable assistance. The responsibility for the interpretation and use of the data - lies, of course, with the author.

This chapter provides a summary of the major findings from the case study data. Detailed accounts of the cases have been published elsewhere (1) and further evidence in support of the general conclusions may be obtained by reference to the author's previous work in the field of work reorganization.(2)

Case study 1: Five-crew shiftworking - A chemical company

The shorter working week - below 40 hours - has led to increased interest in the utilization of 5-crew shiftworking where continuous production is in operation. The chemical industry has a long tradition of shiftworking and in 1984 a national agreement was signed between the employers' association and the trade unions bringing about a 38-hour week. Not all companies in the industry are subject to this agreement but its achievement has had a wide impact with few chemical companies now operating more than a 38-hour week. The company studied was not a member of the employers' association and therefore not subject to the national agreement. However, since its establishemnt in the United Kingdom (the company is foreign-owned), it has sought to establish working conditions and remuneration well in advance of the national agreements for the industry as a whole. The innovation was based on a reduction in the working week from 39 hours to 36 hours accompanied by a movement from 4-crew working to 5-crew working. It was also associated with a major work reorganization exercise and productivity agreement which introduced more flexible working practices and exchanged 8-hour shiftworking for 12-hour shifts.

Summary

The case study had a number of key points:

1. a move to 5-crew shiftworking based on 12-hour shifts providing a specified annual time contract - 142 shifts a year
2. the creation of additional jobs, plus increased productivity and efficiency through work reorganization (flexible working practices) and overtime reduction
3. an internal agreement arranged by both sides at plant-level with little outside stimulus
4. a radically reduced working week (from 39 hours to 36 hours) and the creation of 'longer leisure blocks'
5. a voluntary agreement, with no legal stipulations, which depended on joint co-operation to be fully effective
6. an agreement to which both parties and the workforce appeared to be strongly committed.

Case study 2: Part time working - A textile company

The case study involved the use of part time work to meet adjustments in demand. Operational time had been reorganized to extend production time. The reorganization had been accompanied by a reclassification of part time working which effectively provided a two-tier system of 'permanent' and 'temporary' part timers. The employment regulation of the two groups had been detailed and the means of movement specified. The net result was a more flexible workforce with enhanced job security provisions for the 'permanent' core.

Summary

The company had reorganized its operational time by means of extending its shiftworking arrangements and instituting a two-tier system for its part time employees. Production time had been increased by 50 per cent with consequent potential for a similar increase in output. The workforce had been made more flexible and the company felt better able to respond to market fluctuations. The workforce had negotiated an agreement on the reorganization which had given the core of 'permanent' part timers greater job security and more say in certain areas of manpower planning.

The exercise had not witnessed a major trade-off in regard to rewards - it was not a 'productivity deal' in the accepted sense. However, it was a more subtle alteration of employment conditions, fuelled by the need for the reorganization of operational time, which may be of wider significance. The achievement of a more flexible workforce by the use of 'core' and 'peripheral' groups of workers (in this case 'permanent' and 'temporary') has been commented upon in a number of other contexts. To find it appearing amongst a largely part time workforce is perhaps illustrative of a further trend. The wider implications of this case study will be examined later in the conclusions.

Case study 3: Harmonization - A pharmaceutical company

The case study was conducted at a branch-plant of a multinational pharmaceutical company. The changeover described had been conducted throughout all U.K. plants as part of a national agreement. The reorganization involved a reduction in working time for office workers from 36½ to 36 hours a week and a reduction for manual workers from 38 per cent to 36 hours a week - an effective harmonization of working time for the company's employees.

Summary

The reorganization was aimed at the production workforce. They were most affected by the change but equally they were the major beneficiaries of harmonization. Any misgivings that 'staff' had about harmonization did not materialize during the course of the case study, but that was not the primary focus of attention. The company introduced the scheme at national level with full union agreement but did not conduct any major degree of consultation at local level. The company was committed to a single-move harmonization programme and would not be persuaded otherwise. It achieved harmonization without indulging in a productivity deal and with minimal manpower changes. At plant level, in the case studies, it took the opportunity to reorganize production and appeared to reap the benefits of greater efficiency. Part of this can be attributed to the new patterns of working time introduced and part can be attributed to the changed working conditions which attended them.

Case study 4: Flexible rostering - A study on the railways

In December 1918, the unions and the employers on the railways reached an agreement that an eight-hour day for footplatemen would be introduced from 1 February 1919. The main points of the agreement were that each footplateman was guaranteed at least eight hours pay a day, whether or not there was eight hours work for him to do. If a footplateman's shift exceeded eight hours in length, he was entitled to overtime rates for the time he worked in excess of eight hours. Thus, if a footplateman worked for less than eight hours, he still received eight hours pay, while if he worked for longer than eight hours he received overtime pay.

In 1982 the primary union and the employers reached an agreement of flexible rostering which ended the principle of a guaranteed eight hours pay a day for footplatemen. The union only accepted flexible rostering with great reluctance, after one of the most bitter conflicts the railways have experienced since nationalization. The principle of flexible rostering, or variable day rostering, is that footplatemen's rosters should vary in length to take into account the length of time the footplatemen will actually be working. The 1982 flexible rostering agreement introduced roster work cycles with footplatemen's turns varying between seven and nine hours in length, on the basis of a standard working week of 39 hours. Under flexible rostering, footplatemen's working hours are calculated on the basis of a roster cycle of eight weeks. Over the eight weeks, a footplateman's working hours should average out to 39 hours. Thus, the number of hours a footplateman should work during his eight weeks (excluding overtime working) is 312.

This case study was conducted at a single depot, concerned with passenger trains, where flexible rostering had been introduced. The examination of the reorganization of operational time is therefore somewhat partial but it does provide important lessons in regard to the wider changes discussed elsewhere and in relation to the experiences of innovations in manufacturing described in the other case studies.

Summary

Flexible rostering involved a major exercise in the reorganization of operational time. It was introduced against the wishes of the main union involved following a protracted industrial dispute. It did not have the sympathy of those who had to operate it, who were not consulted as to the form it would take nor were they given any choice in regard to the working patterns to be operated. The case study illustrated some of the difficulties involved at a local depot where the introduction of the new system had been regarded as 'most successful' by management.

As a case in the introduction of 'flexible working hours' the study must be treated with some caution. Both because of its partial nature (one depot in a whole national network) but more importantly because of the partial nature of the innovation itself. Flexible rostering does not fall within the mainstream of 'flexible working hours' innovations as most would understand them. It is more akin to a shiftwork innovation than an example of flexi-time. There are no 'core' hours and no individual choice over daily, weekly, monthly or cyclical hours. Individuals work to an 8-week roster or cycle in much the same way as shiftworkers work to a 4 or 5 week cycle.

The case is interesting mainly for what it may well be a precursor to, rather than what was actually accomplished. There is no doubt that companies will seek to maximize operational time in order to make more efficient use of capital and manpower resources. The way in which this is done could well be a major factor in the degree of success achieved. Where co-operation is sought through prior consultation and a satisfactory agreement reached, the greater the commitment to the change. Where change is imposed against workforce wishes or those of their representatives, the lower the level of commitment. This may appear obvious but the case underlines the point that innovations depend as much on personal and collective motivation as on the neatness of the blueprint. In this case management wanted to break what they felt was an artificial time barrier - the eight-hour day - in order to make for greater efficiency and more productive use of manpower resources. In the long-run they may prove successful. However, in the short-run they appear to have replaced a major barrier by a host of minor barriers. Rigid interpretation of the rules surrounding the new rosters make 'flexible rostering' a misnomer. The scheme involved minor flexibilities narrowly interpreted. It is difficult to perceive who is gaining in the process.

The reorganization of operational time fails if it is seen in terms of 'winners' and 'losers' (as with much of 'flexible rostering'). There has to be a wider spectrum of rewards. Individuals have to be seen to gain something if they are to remain committed to it. It is desirable that a balance exists between costs and benefits. If the benefits to the individual appear minimal, the commitment to making the new system work will operate at a similar level.

Conclusions from case studies

The four case studies analysed are illustrative of some of the major innovations currently taking place in the United Kingdom in regard to the reorganization of operational time at plant level in manufacturing industry. They highlight a range of attempted solutions to a common problem - the need to reorganize working time and working practices in order to increase productivity and efficiency. Common features are trade union/workforce pressure for shorter hours, job security and employment combined with company/managerial pressure for greater flexibility, productivity and output. The clash between the two invariably produces some form of 'trade-off' in regard to the final agreement. In all these cases there was some 'reward' for the workforce either in regard to remuneration, enhanced job security or shorter hours. However, whilst a 'trade-off' of some kind featured in these studies, this is not to say that they are indicative of all work reorganization exercises. It may, nonetheless, be indicative of those reorganizations which can claim to have been a 'success'.

The case study approach has certain methodological limitations as outlined in the introduction. Selectivity and data extrapolation clearly present problems. This was forcefully brought home to the research team when very recently (after the case study work was completed) one of the companies that had been approached to participate in the project - a branch-plant of a multi-national tobacco company which had recently 'harmonized' its working hours for all employees on the basis of a 35-hour week - announced the closure of the factory concerned with the loss of 600 jobs! As well as explaining why the company did not want to participate in the research, it underlines the fact that work reorganization not only involves changes at plant level but also at company level. The vast majority of employees in United Kingdom manufacturing industry work for companies with multi-plant operations. The recession, changes in demand, new technology, rationalization, etc., have all combined to place jobs at risk. In fact nearly 2 million jobs in British manufacturing industry have been 'lost' in the last eight years with insufficient compensatory 'gains'. Plant reorganization may be successfully achieved, productivity improved, only to find that wider corporate strategies place employment in doubt. There is no simple answer to this problem but it does serve to illustrate another limiting factor of the case study approach in that all studies are 'frozen in time'. Today's successful reorganization may be tomorrow's failure (equally current problems, as exemplified in the flexible rostering study, may only be a transitory phenomenon).

Despite its limitations, the case study approach can provide clear evidence of innovative developments which meet a variety of objectives - specifically that combine more efficient and productive working with benefits in regard to working time and conditions. The myth that working time cannot be reduced without a negative effect on costs needs to be exploded and plant-level studies provide a good weapon for that purpose. If working time reductions only ever had a negative effect on costs we would all still be working a 60-70 hour week for 50-52 weeks of the year as did our forebears. Clearly shorter working time and productivity improvements (better use of capital and labour) have gone hand-in-hand. How they can be further advanced needs to be explored at many levels - one of which is that of the firm. The conclusions which this small array of studies offers to this process will now be addressed.

Motivation

The reasons why companies undertake major work reorganization exercises appear to be many and varied. Clearly they are all designed to improve efficiency and make the plants more productive. However, there are other considerations as well. The most obvious consideration is external, trade union, pressure to reduce working hours. Whilst present in the case studies, they did not appear to be a major motivational factor. Even in the shiftworking study, where it was at its most apparent, the company did not bow to pressure so much as utilize the shorter working week in order to obtain an agreement on new working practices. Trade union pressure of itself may not lead to work reorganization, but it can be the catalyst for some kind of trade-off which gives shorter hours as a reward for new arrangements seen as beneficial to the company.

A summary of the motivational factors in the four studies would appear as:

Case study 1 - inefficient shiftworking system plus need for new working practices
Case study 2 - greater flexibility of manpower plus extra shift required
Case study 3 - desire to standardize conditions
Case study 4 - progress demanded on altering traditional practices and arrangements.

The shorter working week was a means to, or a by-product of, the required charges; it was not a primary motivational factor. Further, the need to tackle unemployment by reducing hours did not appear as a factor at all.

Negotiation/adaptation

The processes of change were equally diverse. Case study 1 owed a lot to local conditions (employee desire for 12-hour shifts) but the trade union side were restricted by the company's willingness to ballot the workforce on the changes and hence, to a degree, to go over their heads. Equally, there was strong company-level pressure to introduce more flexible working practices. Case study 2 was a local plant agreement, albeit in a single-plant operation, but the outside full time trade union officer was an important influence over events. In case study 3 the company unilaterally imposed the change and only left to local level how it was to be implemented. Finally, in case study 4, the decision was made at national level and imposed against union wishes. In all cases the unions and workforce representatives were responding to company pressure for change and were not the initiators of it. This could be said to be representative of most work reorganizations (certainly in the United Kingdom).

Despite the managerial origins of the change and strong commitment to it, in cases 1-3 there were elements of positive consultation and negotiation. In these instances a jointly agreed solution, and one to which both sides appeared committed, was the outcome. Only in case study 4 was there a lack of joint commitment and this reorganization encountered the most problems in terms of implementation.

A particular feature common to all four case studies was the strong element of <u>company-level</u> pressure for change. Many work reorganizations involving working time innovations are largely the product of local initiatives, albeit in response to wider company problems/strategies.(3) It would be wrong to generalize from such a small number of case studies but the wider trend discernible in Britain of 'regaining managerial control' may generate greater company-level involvement in the 'nuts and bolts' of plant-level reorganization. Companies may become less inclined to allow plants to find their own solutions to what may be seen to be largely local problems. If this were the case national, industry-wide or company-bargaining may exert greater influence over working time patterns than hitherto. Plant-level flexibility may be sacrificed to meet company-level expectations.

The full industrial relations implications of work reorganization cannot be drawn from such a narrow range of studies. However, there have been many other recent examples in manufacturing industry of companies reorganising operational time in order to alter working practices, particularly to introduce greater elements of flexibility. In many of these cases external trade union representation has been of greater significance than that internally. Further, where obstacles have occurred, there has been a tendency to give employees a choice by ballot as to what working patterns will be introduced. The era of plant-level, shopfloor bargaining characteristic of the 'shop stewards' movement' in manufacturing industry in the 1960s and 1970s, may be on the wane in the less-prosperous 1980s.

Company-level bargaining and the use of shopfloor ballots are two indications of such a trend; and it is interesting that the case studies illustrate aspects of these developments which have been identified by industrial relations practitioners and commentators as operating on a much wider level. If trade union power is moving away from lay representatives to full time officers and company-level bargaining is assuming greater importance (occasionally assisted by employee ballots) this could have a significant effect on the bargaining of working time. Plant-level independence - 'doing it our way' - may be eroded and greater standardization of company practice - a feature of Japanese industrial relations (perhaps not coincidentally) - might emerge.

Time/income/employment/productivity - 'trade-offs'

The concept of 'trade-offs' as a consequence of work reorganization is hardly a new one. The history of industrialization is littered with examples of employees seeking to extract benefits as a result of labour-saving machinery or altered manning arrangements. In fact, it could be argued that the 'trade-off' approach to technological change and work reorganization is the norm - the 'Luddite' (nineteenth century 'machine-breakers') approach being an extremely rare exception. The key questions are invariably not has a trade-off occurred but what kind of trade-off, who benefits (the individual employee, particular groups of workers, the employer, etc.) and to what extent?

In all these case studies some form of 'trade-off' was utilized. Management were not unilaterally imposing work reorganization without any form of compensation to individuals or groups of workers. The impetus to the change was clearly production-orientated - greater productivity/efficiency, expanded production, better utilization of manpower etc. However, the workforces in each of the studies were given a 'carrot' to facilitate the change - albeit a small one in the railways study. The form of the 'carrot' varied but in three of the four cases (all except the part time study - 2) it involved an element of reduced working time (from major in the shiftworking case to relatively minor in the railways study).

Industrial relations commentators, in noting the propensity for firm or company-level trade-offs, have pointed to recent American experience and the practice of 'concession bargaining', which has been seen as a feature of the recession. 'Concession bargaining' has primarily involved the acceptance of low (occasionally zero or even minus) wage increases, agreement to productivity improvements - workforce flexibility etc, in exchange for greater job security for the 'core' workforce and, in some cases, shorter hours. The American automobile and steel industries are quoted as examples of this practice. In Europe there has been less evidence of this type of 'trade-off' and in the United Kingdom very little. In the United Kingdom jobs have been lost, rationalized or 'sold' (depending on one's point of view) in exchange for redundancy payments. Attempts have been made to maintain jobs, e.g. through short-time working, but there are few instances where workforces have agreed to a reduction in their wages or conditions as the price of maintaining jobs. Even the longest struggles against factory closures or major rationalization exercises have always ended with the acceptance of redundancy terms.

Thus, it would be wrong to conclude that some form of 'concession bargaining', in the American sense, was being introduced as an adjunct to work organization. There is little evidence of it. However, there is evidence that workforces are looking to enhance job security and are prepared to see work reorganization as an opportunity to achieve that end. The notions of the development of 'core' and 'peripheral' workforces are based on this evidence. In one sense a 'concession' is involved but it falls more easily into the traditional 'trade-off' via collective bargaining than any other pattern. A number of the case studies illustrate the point - the 'permanent' part time workers achieved greater job security and control by allowing a group of 'temporary' part time workers to be introduced and the chemical workers who moved to five-crew working also believed they had made their own jobs more secure following the agreement.

Case studies 1 and 2 are fairly clear illustrations of 'giving something to get something' - the classic trade-off. In case studies 3 and 4 managerial goals were more long term and less dependent on an exchange of benefits. In the harmonization study the company wanted to give a reward (shorter hours) to a section of its workforce, whilst in the railways study the management were less inclined to give something in return for flexible rostering. A wider range of case studies would probably demonstrate other degrees of employer benefit/employee reward situations. However, despite their diversity, the key element is that some kind of 'trade-off' is usually involved. Change is bargained and bargaining presents an opportunity to alter working conditions to the benefit of all concerned. To what extent these opportunities are grasped remains the key problem.

In Chapter 3 of this report, it was stated that British trade unions have not been that adept at taking the opportunities which work reorganization presents to gain real benefits in terms of jobs and shorter working hours. A dislike of part time working has tended to circumscribe their options in this direction; a hesitancy about shiftworking has produced similar results; and - probably most important of all - a failure or an inability to tackle overtime working. Virtually exclusive concentration on the 'shorter working week' (particularly until 1984) has tended to obscure and frustrate the real objective of shorter working time. Shorter contractual hours and increased overtime working are not a recipe for job creation or efficient production. Concentration on actual hours worked - annual working time - would pay better dividends.

Trade union restrictions on innovations in operational time have been mirrored by equal reluctance on the part of the employers organizations and government to promote such innovations. This reluctance has not prevented innovations occurring, as these and other case studies demonstrate, but it has meant that concepts such as 5-crew shiftworking, annual time contracts, harmonization etc., have not had the kind of publicity which they perhaps deserve. Such innovations can marry the needs of more efficient production with those of shorter working time and, ultimately, jobs. Where they create, save or secure jobs and reduce working time they ought to be highlighted. Constant emphasis on a single objective - be it employers and the need to cut costs or trade unions and the desire to reduce working time - can cloud the fact that both may be achieved by better utilization of manpower. At firm or company-level both sides of industry invariably accept this. It is perhaps at national level where the need for more flexibility in approach is required.

Future trends/innovations

The reorganization of operational time provides opportunities for both sides of the bargaining table. In the United Kingdom, in the foreseeable future, there is little likelihood of state or legislative intervention in regard to reducing working time. Thus what progress that is made will be on a voluntary basis and will almost certainly require the consent of the parties concerned - employers, trade unions and individual employees. These case studies illustrate how some of these opportunities can be taken and also some of the pitfalls involved.

In the future, the main factors in reducing working time will almost certainly not be as a consequence of reducing unemployment. Reducing unemployment may be a beneficial by-product, but it will not be the cause of change. Changes will occur where employers want to make productivity/efficiency improvements and are prepared to consider reduced working time as a possible trade-off. In this regard a number of developments appear to be significant:

1 Longer leisure blocks Either as a consequence of shiftwork innovations or by compressing the working week (4½ and 4 day weeks) - these might include longer shifts or blocks of working time (12 hour and 10 hour shifts): in blue-collar areas (see, for example, case study 1) this is already taking place but it is of interest to note that British tax officers in Birmingham have recently suggested, as part of a reorganization based on new technology, the movement to a 4-day week consisting of 4 x 9¼ hour days - a far longer working day than currently practised (it is of further interest to note that they are proposing doing it as a part of an existing flexi-time agreement which has a 10-hour daily time-band, 8 a.m. to 6 p.m.)

2 Shiftwork innovations Five-crew shiftworking being perhaps the most important for continuous production workers but other innovations, particularly in regard to 'annual time contracts', are also slowly gaining support (again see case study 1 as an example and also case study 3)

3 Harmonization A potentially key development in the United Kingdom where office workers' hours have traditionally been a lot shorter than those of manual workers: the blurring of distinctions between 'blue collar' and 'white collar' facilitated by new microelectronic technology may assist this process (see, for example, case study 3)

4 Part time working Progress here may be dependent on how successful 'job sharing' becomes and what happens to female participation rates as the recession weakens: it is often argued that new technology may provide greater opportunities for women workers and, consequently, an extension of part time working; a key issue affecting this whole subject area is undoubtedly employment rights, protection and job security (see case study 2) - an issue the EEC has sought to promote only to founder on the British veto, and which might re-emerge more strongly under European majority-voting.

5 Flexible working practices/flexi-time At present the drive for more flexible working practices has been mainly levelled at shopfloor, manual, workers and developments in flexi-time have largely occurred among groups of white-collar workers: the spread of the latter into blue-collar areas is possible (see, for example, case study 4 on flexible rostering) although shiftwork may prove a barrier in certain cases; as shopfloor workers come 'off-the-clock' so office workers are going 'on-the-clock' in order to maximize choice over their working and leisure time - a paradoxical situation but one which, in both instances, has potential for reduced working time without impairing productivity.

In regard to the reorganization of operational time, the range of options available is almost infinite. What is limited, in many cases, is the ability or the willingness to set aside traditional practices and experiment with some of these options in pursuit of increased efficiency and shorter working time (i.e. actual rather than contractual). In certain areas, as some of the case studies highlight, movement is taking place and new concepts are being explored. It is in the interests of all that an effective balance is found between maximizing the use of capital equipment in order to generate wealth and increasing the potential for greater leisure time in order to enjoy that wealth, and ensuring that both are more equitably distributed. The case studies of reorganized working time described in this report do not provide the answer to this perennial problem, but they do demonstrate a number of areas in which progress could be made and some of the problems associated with getting there. In that sense it is hoped that they add something to what is an important international as well as national debate.

Notes

1. See P. Rathkey - 'Case Studies in the reorganization of operational time: United Kingdom' in <u>'Reorganisation du Temps de Production'</u> (EIFIP, Brussels, 1985).
2. P. Rathkey - <u>Work sharing and the reduction and reorganization of work at firm level</u> (EEC, Brussels, 1985)
3. See also <u>ibid.</u>

5 Working time preferences

Introduction

One of the major problems facing any study of working time preferences is that of calculation. Are people voting with their feet when they elect to follow a particular work pattern, e.g. female part time workers and male shiftworkers, or is this merely the product of limited choice? Equally, if asked in a vacuum which hours they would prefer to work, much will probably depend on perceived income levels. The question of whether people are prepared to trade income for leisure and, if so, in what proportion is in reality likely to be inextricably linked to the rewards (usually financial) from such work. A good example of this is the proven appeal of job sharing to middle-class, professional women on above average salaries and the lack of appeal of job-splitting to their more lowly paid counterparts. Another example is the ease with which overtime has been bought out in some companies and the great resistance to its erosion among groups of worker whose income levels are heavily reliant on high overtime earnings.

Leaving aside questions of the Protestant work ethic and 'work as social drug' syndrome (both of which are strongly supported by studies of both employed and unemployed), it is at least arguable that many people would wish their working time to be reduced and unquestionable that many people would like a great deal more choice over the hours which they worked and those which they did not. However, in exploring such matters the context of available options (or realistic options) have to be strongly borne in mind, as have the reward systems involved. Equally, there is a clear danger of over-extrapolation from partial data - the circumstances under which people might wish to alter their existing hours are highly individualistic and somewhat loose, or general survey questions do not always provide the answers intended. It is unlikely that the JCF survey completely avoided such pitfalls but attempts were made to sidestep some of the more obvious traps which a number of other studies appeared to have fallen into. (Further details concerning the JCF sample are outlined in Appendix II and the full questionnaire utilized is detailed in Appendix I).

Choosing time contracts

There is a sense in which everybody exercises a degree of choice over their individual working time: at its most basic the choice may appear stark - reduced to whether or not to seek work and/or whether or not to seek full time or part time employment. Few would disagree that choice in this sense is anything other than limited. There are those who opt out of paid employment from choice - the vast majority do not. For the unemployed, particularly males, even the option of part time employment is usually excluded as it is likely to reduce rather than increase total income. Nevertheless, accepting that choice is strictly limited, it is essential to begin an examination of working time preferences by looking at that prescribed range of options. Do we have an army of full time employees desperately seeking part time employment or, more likely, vice versa?

As one might expect, the vast majority of full time employees in the survey, some 91 per cent, worked that way out of choice - see Table 5.1.

Table 5.1
Whether work full time from choice (Q10)
(Base all answering)

	Total	Age				
		16-24	25-34	35-44	45-54	55-64
Total	523	97	142	135	110	39
All (Raw nos.)	253	57	67	60	50	19
Answering (%)	48%	59%	47%	44%	45%	49%
Yes	231	54	62	54	46	15
	91%	95%	93%	90%	92%	79%
No	21	3	4	6	4	4
	8%	5%	6%	10%	8%	21%
Dk/na	1	0	1	0	0	0
	*	-	1%	-	-	-

Equally unsurprising was that about one-third of the sample would expect or might like to work part time in the future see Table 5.2.

Table 5.2
Whether would like/expect to work part time in future

	Total	Age				
		16-24	25-34	35-44	45-54	55-64
All (Raw nos.)	253	57	67	60	50	19
Answering (%)	48%	59%	47%	44%	45%	49%
Yes	80	17	17	16	20	10
	32%	30%	25%	27%	40%	53%
No	159	38	44	41	27	9
	63%	67%	66%	68%	54%	47%
Dk/na	14	2	6	3	3	0
	6%	4%	9%	5%	6%	-

It may be assumed that this might be a considerable way off in the future for some, but for others it could represent a more immediate desire. However, caution must be exercised. A desire to reduce hours in the abstract may say little about preferences in the real world - it is too akin to the sort of scenario that arises out of a 'what would you do if you won the pools' type of question.

Given that few elect to be unemployed and that when in full time work the choices available, such as they are, could be considered to be optimized, it is to be expected that the vast majority of full time employees would see their situation as one born out of choice. If not, why not change or get out? However restricted a person feels, the notion of 'free will' invariably intrudes - to think otherwise involves a degree of self-criticism which most of us seek to avoid. However, for the part time worker such psychological encumbrances do not apply. For the part time worker seeking full time employment no form of self-criticism needs be implied. Here circumstances might be seen to play a much larger part in determining the outcome. Nevertheless, it would appear that the vast majority of part time workers are <u>not</u> frustrated full time employees - see Table 5.3.

Table 5.3
Whether work part time from choice (Q11)

	Total	Age				
		16-24	25-34	35-44	45-54	55-64
Total	109	6	27	36	29	11
Yes	93	1	25	33	25	9
	85%	17%	93%	92%	86%	82%
No	12	4	2	1	3	2
	11%	67%	7%	3%	10%	18%
Dk/na	4	1	0	2	1	0
	4%	17%	-	6%	3%	-

To work part time is a conscious choice within prevailing individual circumstances and for many, particularly after the mid-30s, there is no expectation of a move to full time employment - see Table 5.4.

Table 5.4
Whether would like/expect to work full time in future

	Total	Age				
		16-24	25-34	35-44	45-54	55-64
Yes	34	4	15	8	5	2
	31%	67%	56%	22%	17%	18%
No	67	1	10	25	22	9
	61%	17%	37%	69%	76%	82%
Dk/na	8	1	2	3	2	0
	7%	17%	7%	8%	7%	-

Desire for reduced hours

Knowing that most people choose whether to work full time or part time and that some might consider the other if circumstances obtained, says little about the how, what, where and why of time preferences. Assuming the importance of rewards to choice, a number of studies have posed the alternative of 'better pay for the same hours' versus 'shorter hours for the same pay'. The OECD produced an international preference table on the basis of such a choice - see Table 5.5.

Table 5.5
Choice between either better pay for the same hours or shorter hours for the same pay? (Time/Income Trade-Offs)

	Shorter Hours	Better Pay	Don't Know
Denmark	66	26	8
Netherlands	64	28	8
W. Germany	55	35	10
France	54	41	5
Belgium	53	37	10
United Kingdom	51	45	4
Italy	40	55	5
Ireland	32	61	7

Source: OECD - Labour Supply Growth Constraints and Work Sharing (1982)

A Swedish Ministry of Labour Study, (1) also in the early 1980s, produced a more detailed set of responses from a larger sample to the same question - see Table 5.6.

Age appeared to have a certain significance concerning employee choice. Young men preferred higher wages before shorter working hours - see Table 5.7.

Those who wanted shorter hours were inevitably predominantly full time employees - see Table 5.8.

The JCF sample, albeit smaller than the Swedish, generated a very different response when the identical question was posed. It effectively reversed the 52/38 Swedish equation favouring shorter hours to 38/56 in favour of more money - see Table 5.9.

Table 5.6

Choice between higher wages with fixed working hours and shorter working hours with fixed wages for employees who prefer unchanged weekly working hour length. By full time, part time and sex. Percentage (DELFA)

	Higher wages	Shorter working hours	Don't know	Total	Number (000s)
Full time employees	33.2	58.2	8.6	100.0	2162
Men	35.3	56.0	8.7	100.0	1470
Women	28.7	62.8	8.5	100.0	692
Part time employees	50.7	31.9	17.4	100.0	745
Men	42.4	30.0	27.6	100.0	96
Women	52.0	32.2	15.9	100.0	649
All	37.7	51.4	10.0	100.0	2907
Men	35.7	54.4	9.9	100.0	1565
Women	40.0	48.0	12.1	100.0	1341

Table 5.7

Choice between higher wages with fixed working hours and shorter working hours with fixed wages for full time employees who prefer unchanged weekly working hour length. By sex and age. Percentage (DELFA)

	Higher wages	Shorter weekly working hours	Don't know	Total	Number (000s)
Men	35.3	56.0	8.7	100.0	1470
of which:					
16-24	48.3	44.3	7.4	100.0	209
25-44	36.0	56.0	7.3	100.0	790
45-64	27.4	61.1	11.5	100.0	468
Women	28.7	62.8	8.5	100.0	692
of which:					
16-24	40.9	51.4	7.7	100.0	148
25-44	26.3	67.0	6.7	100.0	339
45-64	24.1	64.4	11.5	100.0	204

Table 5.8

Persons who prefer shorter working hours before higher wages. By sex and normal length of working hours. Percentage (DELFA)

	Normal length of working hours					
	Part time 1-19 hrs	Part time 20-34 hrs	Total part time	Full time	Total	Number (thousands)
Men	0.6	2.8	3.4	96.6	100.0	852
Women	2.4	30.0	32.4	67.6	100.0	643
Both sexes	1.4	14.5	15.9	84.1	100.0	1495

Table 5.9

Whether would work same/less hours for more/same pay (Q14)

Total	523	97	142	135	110	39	77	61	171	120
Higher wages and same hours	291	71	87	59	56	18	47	32	101	57
	56%	73%	61%	44%	51%	46%	61%	52%	59%	48%
Same wages and less hours	198	23	48	64	43	20	28	26	57	57
	38%	24%	34%	47%	39%	51%	36%	43%	33%	48%
Depends how much more/less	11	1	4	2	4	0	0	0	7	2
	2%	1%	3%	1%	4%	-	-	-	4%	2%
Dk/not sure	23	2	3	10	7	1	2	3	6	4
	4%	2%	2%	7%	6%	3%	3%	5%	4%	3%

The conclusions which the OECD and Swedish studies drew was that here was evidence of a strong desire for reduced working hours among possibly over half of the working population. It was not an abstract 'would you like shorter working hours' along the lines of 'are you against sin', but appeared to posit a tangible choice between a higher standard of living versus a lower standard of living with more time in which to enjoy it. If this were the case, it might be argued that substantial opportunities for time-income trade-offs might be opened up. However, a closer examination of the choice on offer might suggest other interpretations.

In this instance, the option of retaining one's present standard of living is retained throughout. However, in reality, this is only likely to occur through piecemeal reductions in working time which are periodically negotiated, such as movement from a 40-hour to a 39-hour week. To ascertain the demand for greater employee choice over hours worked, it is necessary to pose the more difficult alternative of a corresponding decrease in wages in accordance with a reduction in hours. Only by so doing can an effective gauge of feeling towards voluntary reduced time be measured.

The Swedish study did make claims to assess working hours preferences on the basis of such conditions (a reduction in income corresponding to any reduction in hours plus an increase in income from greater hours). Their findings are worth noting - see Table 5.10.

Table 5.10
Preferences concerning changing working hours among part time and full time employees. Men and women. Percentage (DELFA)

	Wish to decrease working hours	Wish to increase working hours	Wish to have un-changed working hours	Total	Number (in thousands)
Full time employees	20.4	2.7	76.8	100.0	2814
Men	17.6	3.1	79.3	100.0	1853
Women	25.9	2.0	72.1	100.0	960
Part time employees	4.7	22.1	73.3	100.0	1016
Men	4.8	22.2	73.1	100.0	131
Women	4.6	22.0	73.3	100.0	885
All Employees	16.3	7.8	75.9	100.0	3830
Men	16.7	4.4	78.9	100.0	1985
Women	15.7	11.6	72.7	100.0	1845

Some 20 per cent of full time employees wishing to reduce their working hours is quite impressive, although it has to be weighed against a similar figure for part time employees who wished to increase their hours (mainly females in the 16-24 age group). Shorter hours were preferred by older full time workers, perhaps not surprisingly - see Table 5.11.

Table 5.11
Preference to decrease working hours. Sex and age. Full time employees. Percentage (percentages indicate the proportion in different age and sex groups who wish to decrease working hours) (DELFA)

Age	Men	Women	Both sexes
16-24	9.9	17.7	13.2
25-44	17.6	28.7	21.2
45-64	20.8	26.8	22.8
65-74	-	-	-
All full time employees	17.6	25.9	20.4

Of those full time employees who wished to reduce their working time and take a corresponding cut in pay, it is interesting to note that over half wished for a reduction in excess of 10 hours a week, i.e. were seeking something halfway between full time and part time work and not just looking to knock a few hours off the working week see Table 5.12.

Table 5.12
Full time employees who prefer to decrease working hours. By sex and preferred increase in working hours. Percentage (DELFA)

	Preferred decrease in number of hours per week							
	1-5 hrs	6-9 hrs	10-13 hrs	14-19 hrs	20 hrs	Information lacking	Total	Number (Thousands)
Men	31.4	21.4	33.4	5.1	7.3	1.4	100.0	326
Women	14.0	22.2	47.0	6.5	9.9	0.3	100.0	249
Both sexes	23.9	21.8	39.3	5.7	8.4	0.9	100.0	574

It is possible to argue, therefore, that meaningful reductions in working hours (say to a 30-hours week) with a corresponding loss of income, might appeal to a significant number (around 10 per cent of the total workforce on these figures) of full time workers in Sweden, if such a choice existed.

However, the British JCF survey sample of 1988 showed nothing like the same propensity to reduce hours when the question was posed to them - see Table 5.13.

Only 6 per cent, compared to 20 per cent, of the total sample were prepared to work less hours for less pay - only 5 per cent of males compared with over 16 per cent in the Swedish sample.

Thus, when standards of living were not presumed to drop, 38 per cent of the British sample appeared to prefer a cut in hours to higher wages, but when hours reductions were equated with lower living standards that outwardly impressive figure dwindled down to a mere 6 per cent. Across a range of variables relating to age, class, sex, number of children, income, full time/part time, occupation, industry, union/non-union, area, accommodation, education, etc, the highest figure recorded was 10 per cent for 55-64 year olds and for C2D females. Very few seemingly, regardless of their position or circumstances, were prepared to exchange income for hours.

Table 5.13
Whether would work more/less hours proportionally to pay (Q13A)

Total	523	97	142	135	110	39	308	215	414	109
Work more hours for more pay	189 36%	46 47%	67 47%	43 32%	29 26%	4 10%	128 42%	61 28%	156 38%	33 30%
Work less hours for less pay	33 6%	3 3%	8 6%	10 7%	8 7%	4 10%	15 5%	18 8%	25 6%	8 7%
Same hours and same pay	260 50%	45 46%	56 39%	70 52%	59 54%	30 77%	143 46%	117 54%	204 49%	56 51%
Not applicable to my job	30 6%	1 1%	8 6%	10 7%	11 10%	0 -	16 5%	14 7%	21 5%	9 8%
Dk/not sure	11 2%	2 2%	3 2%	2 1%	3 3%	1 3%	6 2%	5 2%	8 2%	3 3%

The lack of willingness to exchange income for hours among the sample presents real problems for those associated with V-time initiatives i.e. voluntary reduced working time. V-time advocates have often based their assumptions by posing a prospective wage increase and then costing it against a variety of time options (not dissimilar to the higher wage/same hours versus same wages/shorter hours dichotomy). For example, Best's study in California (2) showed the following results (Table 5.14):

Table 5.14
Worker choice amongst equally costly options (per cent)

Option		1st choice	2nd choice	3rd choice
1	2 per cent pay increase	14.3	19.6	28.7
2	10 minute reduction each day	0.7	3.7	12.0
3	50 minute reduction in 1 day/week	12.2	29.7	28.9
4	Five extra days paid holiday	55.6	24.9	9.6
5	Earlier retirement	17.2	22.2	20.8

Again the difficult question of reduced income is avoided. Other surveys have generated similar results.(3) However, abstract or hypothetical propositions seldom occur around the bargaining table. If rises are foregone then standards of living will drop and there is little evidence from the JCF data that anything representing more than a tiny minority of any given workforce in the United Kingdom in 1988 are prepared to countenance such a drop. This data does not preclude the possibility of reducing working time, it merely argues against some of the more romantic versions of how such a reduction might be achieved.

Any practical approach to working time reduction has to start from the assumption that people do not wish to lower their living standards and income, however desirable increased leisure time might be. The unemployed have limitless 'leisure' but few means. Leisure only becomes truly meaningful when an individual has both the time and the means to enjoy it. Once that is accepted, the possibilities for reduced working time are somewhat restricted, but by no means removed. It might be more convenient for the arguments put forward in this report if the case were different e.g. if the survey results had duplicated those of Sweden. However, it was always unlikely that Swedish employees of the early 1980s - with Sweden having the highest standard of living in Europe - would be replicated in the United Kingdom in the late 1980s. The 'enterprise culture' would appear to allow little room to contemplate a return to the hippie trail - probably for very sensible reasons.

Time use

In order to understand a little more about what greater leisure might be used for were it to become available - the 'carrot' in the shorter working time debate - a variety of options were presented to the sample. This was deliberately presented without reference to income - in other words the fruits of any normal negotiated reduction in working hours or, perhaps, readjustment to working hours (lengthening the working day but reducing the number of days worked might provide more perceived leisure/spare time even though working hours remain the same). The findings are detailed in Table 5.15. Without exploring such usages in

Table 5.15
Usage of spare time if became available (Q19A/B)

	Total	Age						Class					Age/Class				Sex/Class				
		16-24	25-34	35-44	45-54	55-64		AB	C1	C2	D		16-34 C1	16-34 C2D	35-64 C1	35-64 C2D		Male C1	Female C1	Male C2D	Female C2D
Total	523	97	142	135	110	39		94	138	198	93		74 64	129	162		77	61	171	120
Take a second job	43 8%	15 15%	14 10%	6 4%	8 7%	0 -		1 1%	7 5%	21 11%	14 15%		4 3%	25 19%	10 6%		4 5%	3 5%	22 13%	13 11%
Travel	255 49%	47 48%	62 44%	69 51%	56 51%	21 54%		46 49%	74 54%	93 47%	42 45%		35 47% 30 47%	54 42%	81 50%		45 58%	29 48%	82 48%	53 44%
Shopping	86 16%	16 16%	24 17%	21 16%	18 16%	7 18%		16 17%	21 15%	33 17%	16 17%		12 16% 9 14%	21 16%	28 17%		5 6%	16 26%	10 6%	39 33%
Watch television/video	82 16%	18 19%	27 19%	14 10%	19 17%	4 10%		15 16%	18 13%	37 19%	12 13%		10 14% 8 13%	29 22%	20 12%		13 17%	5 8%	34 20%	15 13%
Listen to the radio	40 8%	8 8%	10 7%	10 7%	8 7%	4 10%		12 13%	7 5%	14 7%	7 8%		5 7% 2 3%	11 9%	10 6%		6 8%	1 2%	11 6%	10
Go to the pub	98 19%	26 27%	30 21%	20 15%	16 15%	6 15%		14 15%	23 17%	44 22%	17 18%		13 18% 10 16%	37 29%	24 15%		15 19%	8 13%	45 26%	16 13%
Visit the countryside	178 34%	21 22%	41 29%	50 37%	45 41%	16 41%		40 43%	46 33%	64 32%	28 30%		18 26% 16 27%	42 33%	55 34%		30 39%	16 26%	52 30%	40 33%
Eat out	104 20%	18 19%	27 19%	29 21%	22 20%	8 21%		20 21%	31 22%	35 18%	18 19%		14 19% 17 27%	23 18%	30 19%		17 22%	14 23%	30 18%	29 24%
Aerobics/dancing exercise at home	56 11%	11 11%	23 16%	18 13%	4 4%	0 -		17 18%	15 11%	14 7%	10 11%		12 16% 3 5%	10 8%	14 9%		7 9%	8 13%	3 2%	21 18%
Playing/being with children	135 26%	12 12%	52 37%	42 31%	24 22%	5 13%		33 35%	37 27%	44 22%	21 23%		20 27% 17 27%	30 23%	35 22%		25 32%	12 20%	45 26%	20 17%
Go to cinema	84 16%	19 20%	21 15%	20 15%	16 15%	8 21%		25 27%	23 17%	26 13%	10 11%		16 22% 7 11%	15 12%	21 13%		13 17%	10 16%	17 10%	19 16%
Cooking for pleasure	76 15%	13 13%	16 11%	22 16%	16 15%	9 23%		14 15%	20 14%	27 14%	15 16%		8 11% 12 19%	18 14%	24 15%		6 8%	14 23%	8 5%	34 28%
DIY	138 26%	17 18%	42 30%	35 26%	31 28%	13 33%		29 31%	27 20%	60 30%	22 24%		15 20% 12 19%	34 26%	48 30%		19 25%	8 13%	60 35%	22 18%
Entertaining friends at home	150 29%	35 36%	40 28%	35 26%	29 26%	11 28%		35 37%	45 33%	46 23%	24 26%		24 33% 21 33%	36 28%	34 21%		18 23%	27 44%	31 18%	39 33%
Go to betting shop	10 2%	3 3%	4 3%	2 1%	1 1%	0 -		1 1%	0 -	5 3%	4 4%		3 4% 0 -	6 5%	3 2%		3 4%	0 -	9 5%	0 -
Go to bingo hall	8 2%	3 3%	3 2%	1 1%	1 1%	0 -		0 -	1 1%	3 2%	3 3%		1 1% 1 2%	3 2%	2 1%		0 -	2 3%	1 1%	4 3%
Gardening	183 35%	14 14%	50 35%	57 43%	43 39%	19 49%		37 39%	41 30%	74 37%	31 33%		17 23% 24 38%	36 28%	69 43%		21 27%	20 33%	62 36%	43 36%
Home computer	43 8%	8 8%	13 9%	10 7%	7 6%	5 13%		14 15%	10 7%	11 6%	8 9%		7 8% 5 8%	9 7%	4 4%		7 9%	3 5%	17 10%	2 2%
Read books	158 30%	20 21%	36 25%	47 35%	38 35%	17 44%		37 39%	42 30%	55 28%	24 26%		19 26% 23 36%	51 39%	31 19%		21 27%	21 34%	29 17%	50 42%
Read newspapers/general magazines	117 22%	14 14%	32 23%	30 22%	27 25%	14 36%		31 33%	26 19%	39 20%	21 23%		12 16% 14 22%	28 22%	35 22%		12 16%	14 23%	39 23%	21 18%
Play individual sports	139 27%	33 34%	48 34%	39 29%	15 14%	4 10%		35 37%	43 31%	44 22%	17 18%		28 38% 23 36%	15 12%	25 15%		16 23%	10 16%	44 26%	17 14%
Play team sports	93 18%	25 26%	39 27%	17 13%	9 8%	4 10%		14 15%	36 26%	30 15%	13 14%		24 32% 19 29%	12 9%	12 7%		27 35%	9 15%	37 22%	6 5%
Watch sports	121 23%	19 20%	41 29%	25 19%	26 24%	10 26%		19 20%	34 25%	47 24%	21 23%		19 26% 15 23%	15 12%	32 20%		28 36%	6 10%	62 36%	6 5%
Studying	60 11%	16 16%	16 11%	16 12%	10 9%	2 5%		23 24%	17 12%	14 7%	6 6%		13 18% 4 6%	4 3%	13 8%		9 12%	8 13%	11 6%	5 5%
Dk/na	11	1	1	0	0	0		1 1%	1 -	7 4%	6 6%		18 10%	7 4%			0 -	0 -	0 -	9 8%
		1%	1%																	

any great depth, it is of interest to note that 'take a second job' was selected by a mere 8 per cent of the total sample (9 per cent of male and 7 per cent of female : 7 per cent of full time and 12 per cent of part time). Choice of a second job did correlate marginally to income - the lower paid the more likely to select it (some 12 per cent of those with less than £480 a month income chose it), but hardly amounted to a significant number of the sample classification population. The notion that maximization of income was a common let alone a universal goal would not appear to be the case. People would seek opportunities in their jobs to expand income through additional hours but rarely by pursuing second jobs. A significant proportion of people are interested in reduced hours and more leisure time, but seldom at the expense of living standards. The establishment and understanding of such parameters is very important to the examination of policy options in this field.

Extra working hours

As has been noted, some 36 per cent of the JCF sample wanted to 'work more hours for more pay' as opposed to the same hours or even less hours for less pay. However, nearly half of those (45 per cent) only wanted between 1 and 5 hours a week overtime and only 22 per cent actually wanted in excess of 10 hours a week.

Thus, from the sample less than 8 per cent of the total actually wanted, given the choice, to work in excess of 10 hours a week overtime. This at a time when the average overtime per overtime worker in manufacturing industry is very close to 10 hours a week (9.3) - see Table 5.16.

The conclusion to be drawn might be that overtime is nowhere near as popular as is commonly presumed and that voluntary, or even legislative, attempts to control it might not prove as unpopular as many presume. The British worker might not be as keen as their Swedish or foreign counterpart to trade income for leisure, but nevertheless does not appear to be as money-orientated as a cursory look at general time/income options would appear to suggest. The opportunities for working time innovations which seek to reduce time whilst at the same time increasing efficiency, hence guaranteeing earnings if not increasing them, might well be wider than first thought. (For a more detailed analysis of overtime see Chapter 6).

Which route to shorter hours?

There are many ways of reducing hours and detailed discussion of a number of options will be reserved for Chapters 7 and 8. The Swedish study suggested that for those who were seeking shorter hours the preferred route was the 'shorter working week' - chosen by nearly 58 per cent, of whom about half wanted time taken off each day - as against longer holidays and earlier retirement - see Table 5.17.

The British JCF survey offered the same three choices to the full sample and a somewhat different set of results emerged - see Table 5.18.

Instead of nearly 60 per cent preferring the shorter working week, less than 25 per cent did! The most popular of the three options was 'longer holidays', particularly among the young and female. Earlier retirement gained in popularity with the age of the sample, as one might expect, and it was equally favoured by the trade union members in the sample. Even within such a limited range of options, the survey findings do question whether collective bargaining priorities have mirrored individual wishes. It might be thought from this data that strategies designed to generate longer leisure blocks and a shorter working lifetime would have the highest priority. In fact, the opposite has been the case - the 'shorter working week' has been the primary goal to which everything else has been largely subservient (as was detailed in Chapter 3). The implications of this apparent contradiction will be examined more fully in Chapters 7 and 8 where a number of policy options will be explored in greater depth. However, before turning to such policy options, it is necessary to take a closer look at the wider choices between full time and part time employment and the perceived villain of the piece in regard to reduced working hours - overtime.

Table 5.16
How many extra hours would work per week (Q13B)
(Base all work more hours for more pay)

	Total	Age				
		16-24	25-34	35-44	45-54	55-64
Total	189	46	67	43	29	3
1-5	83	24	29	17	11	1
	45%	52%	42%	39%	37%	25%
6-10	58	14	22	13	8	1
	31%	30%	33%	30%	28%	25%
11-15	18	3	5	7	3	0
	10%	7%	7%	16%	10%	-
16-20	11	1	6	2	2	0
	6%	2%	9%	5%	7%	-
20+	11	3	5	0	2	1
	6%	7%	7%	-	7%	25%
Dk/na	8	1	0	4	3	0
	4%	2%	-	9%	10%	-

Table 5.17

Full time employees who prefer shorter working hours before higher wages. By how they wish to shorten their working hours. Sex, age and children. Percentage (DELFA)

	Fewer working hours per week	of which fewer working hours each day	Longer holidays	Lowered pension age	Other	Total	Number (000s)
Men	53.6	27.1	26.3	14.4	5.7	100.0	823
of which:							
16-24 years	61.4	33.5	32.5	2.3	3.8	100.0	93
25-44 years	55.8	28.5	28.5	9.4	6.3	100.0	443
45-64 years	47.5	22.7	20.9	26.1	5.5	100.0	286
Women	66.0	35.1	18.3	10.0	5.7	100.0	435
of which:							
16-24 years	66.0	38.0	28.2	0.8	4.9	100.0	76
25-44 years	69.7	38.6	18.3	6.2	5.9	100.0	227
45-64 years	59.6	27.4	12.5	21.8	6.1	100.0	131
Men with children under seventeen years	56.3	28.7	24.9	12.5	6.4	100.0	359
Men with children under seven years	59.6	32.6	23.8	8.7	7.9	100.0	177
Women with children under seventeen years	71.5	43.0	13.7	7.9	6.9	100.0	142
Women with children under seven years	76.2	49.2	13.3	3.7	6.8	100.0	55
ALL	57.9	29.9	23.5	12.9	5.7	100.0	1258

Table 5.18
Ways in which number of hours could be reduced (Q12)

	Total	16-24	25-34	35-44	45-54	55-64	Male	Female	Full time	Part time	Yes	No
		----------Age----------					----Sex----		--Working--		T.U. member	
Total	523	97	142	135	110	39	308	215	414	109	206	317
Shorter hours each week	121 23%	19 20%	37 26%	31 23%	24 22%	10 26%	75 24%	46 21%	100 24%	21 19%	54 26%	67 21%
Same hours each week with longer holidays	200 38%	54 56%	59 42%	46 34%	32 29%	9 23%	101 33%	99 46%	155 37%	45 41%	57 28%	143 45%
Same hours each week with earlier retirement	149 28%	19 20%	41 29%	40 30%	35 32%	14 36%	112 36%	37 17%	131 32%	18 17%	79 38%	70 22%
None	44 8%	3 3%	5 4%	16 12%	16 15%	4 10%	14 5%	30 14%	21 5%	23 21%	14 7%	30 9%
Dk/not sure	10 2%	2 2%	1 1%	2 1%	3 3%	2 5%	7 2%	3 1%	8 2%	2 2%	2 1%	8 3%

Notes

1. Delfa Project, Swedish Ministry of Labour - <u>Preferred working hours</u> (Delfa Debate Report No. 3 Stockholm 1984)
2. F. Best, 'Preferences on Worklife Scheduling and Work Leisure Trade-offs', <u>Monthly Labour Review</u>, June 1978, (pp. 31-37) p. 33
3. A major American survey found an overwhelming majority of American workers willing to forego much of their future pay rises for more time away 'if some choice is allowed concerning the specific form of potential free time'. Scheduling of free time was all important and there was a clear preference for longer holidays and sabbatical leave rather than the shorter working week. See 'Exchanging Earnings for Leisure: Findings of an Exploratory National Survey ofr Working Time Preference', United States Department of Labor, Washington D.C., 1980, quoted in Armstrong, P., <u>Technical Change and Reductions in Life Hours of Work,</u>Technical Change Centre, London, 1984.

6 Varying hours – part time work, job sharing and overtime

A Part time work

There are over 5 million part time workers in Britain, representing nearly a quarter of the total working population. In the 30 years between 1951 and 1981 there was an overall increase of 1.4 million in the working population, but this rise was entirely due to the boom in part time jobs - an additional 3.7 million (3 million men and 700,000 men). Full time jobs fell by 2.3 million (1.9 million men and 400,000 women). A leading expert in the field has concluded that:

> '... the shift in employment structure springs from newly developed patterns of working hours which do not afford opportunities for the unemployed, and have been met by extending labour supply through increasing the labour force participation of women.' (Robinson, 1985, also source for above figures).(1)

The latest employment figures indicate the scope of that extension - see Table 6.1.

According to a recent CBI survey, it is likely that the proportion of part time workers will continue to increase - particularly among major employers - see Table 6.2.

During 1985, according to the Manpower Services Commission, the number of male employees remained unchanged whilst female employment grew by 167,000 - of which all but 6,000 was due to an increase in the number of women working part time.

Table 6.1
The growth of part time work in Great Britain, 1951-1987

	Total in employment	Full time employment	Part time employment	Part time as per cent of all employment
1951	22,135	21,304	831	4%
1961	23,339	21,272	2,066	9%
1971	23,733	19,828	3,904	16%
1981(A)	22,881	18,977	3,905	17%
1981(B)	23,754	18,871	4,883	21%
1987	24,229	18,646	5,583	23%

Source: Department of Employment

Table 6.2
CBI: Expanding use of part time working 1985-1989

	Net proportion of employers expecting an increase against those expecting a decrease in the proportion of part timers
	Per cent
Manufacturing industries	+8
Other industries	+15
All employers	+13
Employers with 5,000+ employees	+26

To government, it would appear, part time employment is something to be encouraged - lower unit costs, increased labour market flexibility and all that. To trade unions, part time work has traditionally been viewed as cheap labour and - although occasionally more subtly put - 'women's work'. They have until very recently been extremely reluctant to place any priority on the recruitment or betterment of part time workers (part of the problem lies in the lack of women full time officials in the major unions). The consequence has been low unionization rates and poor employment terms and conditions even when unionized.

The spread of part time work outside of the main categories - into banking, insurance, office work, security, hospitals, local authorities etc - has been largely a product of labour demand rather than supply (although most part time workers are not seeking full time employment). At present 10 per cent of local authority education department workers have weekly hours of less than 15, and 50 per cent of ancillary assistants in schools work no more than 16 hours a week. School meals services and cleaning are predominantly part time and domestic assistants in hospitals are nearly all on short-hours contracts. Many of these areas are traditional employers of part time labour but there is a clear growth in the use of part timers.

Part time work and employment

One of the major aspects of work redistribution which requires analysis is the degree of job 'rights' which attaches to the new working pattern. If employees in a firm decide to cut their hours and/or earnings out of choice, then the nature of the job might be largely unaffected. If, however, full time work is converted into part time work, with little or no choice involved and with a loss of job 'rights', then the job itself will have been materially affected. Part time workers are often the first to be made redundant. Would an increase in part time working create jobs or would it largely bring back into the labour market women who presently do not figure in the unemployment statistics? In considering these matters emphasis has to be placed on the fact that traditionally part time working has been concentrated in a limited number of economic sectors, and often it has been associated with low pay, job insecurity, poor employment conditions and sexual divisions of labour.(2) In any discussion of creating jobs through an extension of part time working, these issues are the first which must be debated. The evidence points to the view that, whilst there is plenty of scope for greater part time work, its increase will have only a marginal effect on unemployment.(3) It has social and economic pluses and minuses but it cannot be seen as a realistic substitute for full time work. The nature of Britain's benefits system and the sexual stereotyping of domestic responsibilities will continue to make part time working attractive to certain sections of the workforce. However, policy options designed to tackle the problem of long term unemployment by means of part time working (outside of job sharing) are very narrow and restrictive and in some cases socially undesirable.

Part time work is on the increase in Western Europe. Britain has traditionally had comparatively high levels of part time work and, despite the relative severity of the economic recession, still does. Part time work in Britain, however, is almost exclusively a female preserve - 94 per cent of all part time workers are female.(4) Thus, as some 47 per cent of all female employees work part time, discussion of part time work cannot be disassociated from the discussion of the sexual division of labour. A certain paradox has been noted in a French study concerning part time workers - it appears that women in upper income household brackets prefer part time work, but the bulk of part time work is done by women from households with modest or average incomes.(5)

Short of an intolerable level of state regulation (which in itself would probably break equal opportunities legislation), it is unquestionable that the encouragement or extension of part time working is inevitably the encouragement and extension of either female participation rates or increasing levels of part time working among females already in work. It is doubtful whether a government wishing to reduce unemployment would seek to encourage female participation rates, knowing that many (if not most) of those who would be drawn into the labour market would not be registered as unemployed in the first place. Hence, the development of part time work as a solution to unemployment would seem to revolve around getting full time female employees to work part time or that new opportunities for female workers should be predominantly part time and should be the reserve of those registered as unemployed. The former (unless by means of voluntary choice) is plainly discriminatory - male workers can be put on short-time or even made redundant but there has been little suggestion that a long term solution would be a reversal to part time working. The latter likewise, unless it is suggested that new employment opportunities in predominantly male areas of work should be only open to part time workers.(6) Thus, there are clear social problems involved at the outset, particularly in the light of equal opportunities legislation.

Increasing female participation in the labour market has lead to the development of part time working. The trend is irreversible (despite calls to return to the kitchen and the home) and is recognized as such even by governments who do not fully approve. As nearly 100 per cent of adult males will seek entry into the labour market, a rising proportion of adult females seeking entry poses a major problem when employment opportunities are restricted. It causes even more of a problem when it is suggested that many of the job opportunities created by the new technology will be more 'suitable' to female operatives.(7) The rising tide of women workers threatens male job opportunities as well as traditional male employment preserves. The growth of service industries, the decline of 'heavy' industry (e.g. steel and shipbuilding), the development of new technology and a plethora of social factors all continue to make definite - rather than even probable - increasing female participation rates. Is the extension of part time working a solution to the problem?

In simple economic and employment terms, the case for extending female job opportunities by means of the development of part time working appears to be a strong one. Part time workers tend to be employed in low-paid and low-skilled occupations (pay probably has a stronger correlation with sex than the level of skill involved). The return on employment for economic cost (subsidy or incentive) entailed would probably be higher than any other comparable attempt at job creation i.e. leaving aside for the present its social desirability). This high employment return/low economic investment equation has focused academic and legislative minds on practical policies in this area.(8) In Britain a modest attempt at encouraging part time work has been made under the government's new Community Programme initiatives.(9) Approved schemes may pay up to £60 a week but must pay 'the rate for the job'. For adult workers, unless the going rate is very low, this means that the bulk of individuals on any one scheme must be part time (the subsidy is £60 a head regardless of whether a person works full time or part time).

Trade unions have generally been hostile to part time work - viewing it as cheap labour with few employment rights. However, there are a number of recent cases to suggest that union attitudes are thawing a little - the need for union subscriptions proving a strong counter-argument to traditional opposition. Trade unions are showing greater interest in securing better employment protection and rights for part timers and this could well reflect a growing recognition that part time work is not only here to stay but is a growth area. The growth of white collar unionism and its increasing influence at the TUC will undoubtedly have its effect on attitudes to working practices, although it is extremely unlikely that part time work will ever be embraced with any enthusiasm. In the long term much will depend upon female influence within the trade union movement itself.

It has been estimated that Britain will have 7 million part timers by the year 2007; the equivalent of 28 per cent of the expected employed population.(10) This would represent an increase of around 10 per cent on present figures - a sizeable shift. It is further to be expected that this rise will predominantly be a consequence of higher female participation rates rather than a growth in male part time employment. The question remains whether this trend ought to be encouraged or, possibly, discouraged.

Part time work and employee preferences

There is a danger in discussing part time work that evidence of low pay and poor employment rights leads to the conclusion that here is a exploited section of the workforce whose preferences would strongly favour something different were they to be less exploited. That part time workers are dissatisfied or disgruntled with their lot and eager to discard their 'peripheral' status for the benefit of full time employment. No doubt many would wish that they were better paid and protected. However, attitudes to part time working are often based on misconceptions of what individual part time workers are seeking in their employment. The JCF survey attempted to cast some light on comparative perceptions of work between full time and part time employees and to explore in more detail what their respective preferences were, should choice be widened.

The popular misconceptions regarding part time work are that the work is invariably low-paid, boring, unrewarding and that women work for 'pin money' in exploited circumstances with few employment rights. Where evidence is cited that part time workers appear to choose that form of employment (see Figure 5.3 and Table 5.4), then this is seen to be the product of limited choice or determined circumstances. None of this can be entirely discounted nor does the survey provide conclusive evidence to the contrary. However, certain interesting findings did emerge from the respective samples of full time and part time employees in the sample.

Firstly, there were comparatively more 'dissatisfied' wager-earners in the full time sample (36 per cent) than those working part time (25 per cent) and more 'satisfied' part timers with their wages (60 per cent) than full timers (47 per cent) - see Table 6.3.

Table 6.3
Satisfaction with basic wage (Q5)

		Total	Working Full time	Working Part time
Total		523	414	109
More than satisfied	(+5)	42 8%	34 8%	8 7%
Quite satisfied	(+4)	221 42%	163 39%	58 53%
Neither/nor	(+3)	84 16%	68 16%	16 15%
Less than satisfied	(+2)	113 22%	95 23%	18 17%
Very dissatisfied	(+1)	61 12%	52 13%	9 8%
Dk/na		2 *	2 *	0 -
Mean		3.13	3.08	3.35
Std. err.		.052	.060	.105
Err. var.		.003	.004	.011

Equally, when it came to job interest and job satisfaction, the part timers scored more positively than their full time counterparts – see Tables 6.4 and 6.5.

Table 6.4
How interesting job is (Q3)

		Total	Working Full time	Working Part time
Total		523	414	109
Very interesting	(+4)	168	135	33
		32%	33%	30%
Fairly interesting	(+3)	274	209	65
		52%	50%	60%
Pretty boring	(+2)	64	56	8
		12%	14%	7%
Very boring	(+1)	15	12	3
		3%	3%	3%
Dk/na		2	2	0
		*	*	–
Mean		3.14	3.13	3.17
Std. err.		.032	.037	.065
Err. var.		.001	.001	.004

Table 6.5
How satisfying job is (Q2)

		Total	Working Full time	Working Part time
Total		523	414	109
Very satisfying	(+4)	134	100	34
		26%	24%	31%
Quite satisfying	(+3)	269	217	52
		51%	52%	48%
Not particularly satisfying	(+2)	89	69	20
		17%	17%	18%
Not at all satisfying	(+1)	28	25	3
		5%	6%	3%
Dk/na		3	3	0
		1%	1%	–
Mean		2.98	2.95	3.07
Std. err.		.035	.040	.075
Err. var.		.001	.002	.006

The image of dissatisfied, disinterested workers involved in unrewarding repetitive tasks did not appear to correspond with their own perceptions. When it came to the hours which they were said to enjoy most, the part time sample appeared to be happier in work than their full time counterparts – enjoying combined work and non-work hours to a greater extent – see Table 6.6.

Table 6.6
Hours enjoyed most (Q4)

	Total	Working Full time	Part time
Total	523	414	109
Hours at work	29	23	6
	6%	6%	6%
Hours outside work	236	197	39
	45%	48%	36%
Both equally	254	190	64
	49%	46%	59%
Don't know/na	4	4	0
	1%	1%	-

Although difficult to prove, it might well be argued that the fewer the hours worked the more satisfaction and enjoyment obtained. That long hours breeds dissatisfaction more than does the assumed disadvantages of part time work. In the sample, some part timers worked regularly at weekends - the service industries, particularly retail, moving to 7-day working - but most did not (See Table 6.7).

Table 6.7
How often weekends worked (Q6)

	Total	Working Full time	Part time
Total	523	414	109
Every weekend	73	54	19
	14%	13%	17%
Most weekends	93	88	5
	18%	21%	5%
Occasional weekends	155	143	12
	30%	35%	11%
Never work weekends	199	126	73
	38%	30%	67%
Dk/not sure	3	3	0
	1%	1%	-

Average working hours varied with the majority of part timers working between 15 and 22 hours, with some 25 per cent below 15 hours - see Table 6.8.

Opportunities for overtime were fewer than their full time counterparts, despite the shorter hours worked, and those that did have overtime opportunities tended to have less hours involved (80 per cent of those part timers who had overtime opportunities involved 5 hours or less whereas some 43 per cent of full timers with overtime opportunities had the chance to work 6 hours or more per week) - See Tables 6.9 and 6.10.

Table 6.8
Number of hours worked per week (before overtime)

	Total	Working Full time	Part time
Total	523	414	109
Under 3 hours	1	1	0
	*	*	-
4 - 6 hours	3	0	3
	1%	-	3%
7 - 10 hours	14	1	13
	3%	*	12%
11 - 14 hours	13	2	11
	2%	*	10%
15 - 18 hours	13	0	13
	2%	-	12%
19 - 22 hours	44	1	43
	8%	*	39%
23 - 26 hours	10	1	9
	2%	*	8%
27 - 30 hours	15	12	3
	3%	3%	3%
31 - 34 hours	6	6	0
	1%	1%	-
35 - 38 hours	138	137	1
	26%	33%	1%
39 - 42 hours	166	165	1
	32%	40%	1%
43 - 46 hours	16	16	0
	3%	4%	-
47 - 50 hours	17	17	0
	3%	4%	-
51+ hours	13	13	0
	2%	3%	-
Dk/na	54	42	12
	10%	10%	11%
Mean	34.72	39.17	17.68

Table 6.9
Opportunity for paid overtime (Q7A)

	Total	Working Full time	Part time
Total	523	414	109
Yes	256	211	45
	49%	51%	41%
No	260	198	62
	50%	48%	57%
Dk/na	7	5	2
	1%	1%	2%

Table 6.10
Details of paid overtime (Q7B/C)
(Base all have opportunity to work paid overtime)

	Total	Working Full time	Working Part time
Total	256	211	45
How often have opportunities:			
Every week	81	75	6
	32%	36%	13%
Most weeks	49	39	10
	19%	18%	22%
Occasional weeks	124	96	28
	48%	45%	62%
Dk/na	2	1	1
	1%	*	2%
How many hours paid overtime worked:			
None	34	25	9
	13%	12%	20%
1 - 5 hours per week	122	95	27
	48%	45%	60%
6 - 10 hours per week	62	55	7
	24%	26%	16%
11 - 15 hours per week	17	16	1
	7%	8%	2%
16 - 20 hours per week	9	8	1
	4%	4%	2%
20+ hours per week	8	8	0
	3%	4%	-
Dk/na	4	4	0
	2%	2%	-

Thus, part timers could do little more than add a few extra hours a week to their already limited working time, whereas full timers tended to have greater opportunities to extend their working hours. In one sense this was a product of limited opportunities but, equally, it was a consequence of choice - nearly 60 per cent of the part time sample did not want any overtime a week, compared to only 38 per cent of full timers, and only 7 per cent of the part time sample wanted to increase their hours by more than 10 a week. Thus, very few part time workers wanted or desired full time employment and nor did they wish to work excessive amounts of overtime - see Table 6.11.

Where contractual working hours had changed, either increased or decreased, part timers were more likely to feel that it was a personal choice - particularly where decreased hours were concerned - see Tables 6.12 and 6.13.

None of this survey evidence amounts to verifiable certainties, but it does run counter to the image of women driven into low-paid, unsatisfying work out of some kind of tightly circumscribed set of circumstances. Work is seldom a matter of total free choice but within its limitations there is little evidence here that part timers have even greater limitations thrust upon them then their full time counterparts - in fact most points to the contrary. This does have important policy considerations.

Table 6.11
How many hours paid overtime would choose per week (Q8)

	Total	Working Full time	Working Part time
Total	523	414	109
None	220	157	63
	42%	38%	58%
1 - 5 hours per week	123	98	25
	24%	24%	23%
6 - 10 hours per week	111	97	14
	21%	23%	13%
11 - 15 hours per week	30	28	2
	6%	7%	2%
16 - 20 hours per week	19	14	5
	4%	3%	5%
20+ hours per week	16	16	0
	3%	4%	-
Dk/na	4	4	0
	1%	1%	-

Table 6.12
Details of contracted hours (Q9)

	Total	Working Full time	Working Part time
Total	523	414	109
Who decided hours should change (base all said increased)			
All answering	78	65	13
	15%	16%	12%
Self	29	23	6
	37%	35%	46%
Trade Union	0	0	0
	-	-	-
Employer	44	38	6
	56%	58%	46%
Other	6	5	1
	8%	8%	8%
Dk/na	1	0	1
	1%	-	8%

Table 6.13
Details of contracted hours (Q9)

	Total	Working Full time	Working Part time
Total	523	414	109
Who decided hours should change (Base all said decreased)			
All answering	52	37	15
	10%	9%	14%
Self	18	8	10
	35%	22%	67%
Trade union	13	13	0
	25%	35%	-
Employer	21	18	3
	40%	49%	20%
Other	2	0	2
	4%	-	13%
Dk/na	0	0	0
	-	-	-

Pros and cons

There seems little merit in discouraging the growth of part time work. In fact the contrary might be argued. As attitudes concerning domestic responsibilities, particularly child care, are likely to change a lot more slowly than those concerning the acceptability of women at work across a far wider range of occupations, it seems probable that many women seeking to enter or re-enter the labour market will wish to do so in a part time capacity.(11) Part time work is likely to become increasingly available in low-skilled occupations and the major debate centres on the conditions under which part time workers are employed, particularly employment rights.

The question of whether or not there ought to be a positive incentive to employ people part time is not so simple.(12) It can be argued that more flexible working patterns and greater opportunities for work and income are beneficial both to the individual and to the family unit, certainly the EEC has been a strong advocate of the encouragement of more male involvement in part time work as well as seeing potential employment benefits from its more widespread application.(13) However, the fact remains that increased part time work effectively means increased female part time employment. Is this good or bad? The answer depends on short and long term objectives. In the long term the analysis of Gershuny is undoubtedly accurate:

> ... the only way women's position in the paid workforce can be improved is by redistributing work in the household. (14)

However, that has a certain 'come the revolution' ring to it. It may be that increasing female part time work will prove a step in the direction of the redistribution of household work, although the evidence is sketchy.(15)

In the short term the case requires closer analysis. There can be little doubt that regarding the working hours/employment debate, the advocacy of the promotion of part time working in isolation is straightforwardly discriminatory. Any initiative would unquestionably be aimed, in the first instance, at female blue-collar workers i.e. the lower paid and less-skilled. These women work on average 1 hour a week of overtime.(16) Their male counterparts, in the depths of recession, work on average about 5 hours a week overtime and half of all male blue-collar workers have overtime hours of around 10 a week. The suggestion that future female job opportunities at the lower end of the scale should revolve around the provision of 'one-half' or even 'one-third' jobs, when half their male counterparts continue to perform 'one-and-a-quarter' jobs each, appears, on the surface at least, to be a trifle equivocal. The view that little can be done about overtime but quite a lot can be done about dividing jobs is clearly inconsistent. Part time work is the easier option because it is cheaper and causes fewer problems. However, it will leave unaffected the bedrock of long term male unemployed and it may well only have a marginal impact on female unemployment.(17) It is highly overrated as the prime candidate to tackle unemployment in the sphere of working time, (18) although it has to be recognized that simply because a person is not registered as 'unemployed' does not mean that they are any the less unemployed than somebody who is. Part time work may well have beneficial aspects in terms of widening employment and income among groups who form part of the present day 'hidden unemployed'.(19)

A legislative framework to promote part time work which gave equal attention to the protection of part time workers' employment rights would prove to be socially progressive. Its constituent elements, however, would need far greater attention than has hitherto been afforded. The extent to which it was beneficial to female job opportunities and not just plain discriminitory would largely depend on the package of 'job rights' which went with it.

The EEC has sought to strengthen the rights of part time workers (a move which Britain vetoed). Strengthening part time workers' rights would do much to bring it more securely into the formal economy.(20) As long as it dwells on the shores of the informal economy, it will continue to operate at the margins. Initiatives to provide greater opportunities for male workers to elect to work part time could be explored. It could prove a tangible option, particularly to male workers approaching retirement. The proper context in which to explore that option ought to be a strengthened form of part time work which conferred adequate rights and benefits. Trade-offs between leisure and income tend at present to be the luxury of the better paid. For the unemployed, the low paid and for some part time workers, the options are extremely limited where they exist at all. Nevertheless, the image of part time workers as a 'captive workforce' with poor pay and rewards from work appears plainly false - part time workers do not themselves see it in such a light. They appear to exercise more choice over their patterns of work than their full time colleagues and gain as much if not more from work in the process.

B Job sharing

Job sharing is the voluntary agreement of two people to perform one job, each sharing the same employment rights and all of the benefits. The voluntary aspect is crucial as the purpose is the redistribution of work, with the attendant benefits in terms of shorter working time for the individuals concerned, through the creation of real jobs. Despite the obvious problems involved, the benefits of job sharing have been well-chronicled.(21) These benefits, however, have not been sufficient to make a major impression on employers and trade unions. Initiatives have been circumscribed by suspicion and doubts concerning the objectives of particular schemes.(22) To what extent can particular schemes be seen as voluntary, a product of choice: who should share work and with whom should they share it?(23) Once compulsion is introduced, the object is defeated.

Job sharing and job splitting

Whereas job sharing is a voluntary process, job splitting is the compulsory (and subsidized) division of one job between two people with neither obtaining the employment rights of the original job.(24) Job sharing and job splitting have, for all their apparent similarities, different aims and objectives and, in practice, operate quite differently. Job sharing, as a voluntary exercise with obvious employment creation potential (both sharers have 'real' jobs and do not trouble either social security or the unemployment figures – unlike certain part time or seasonal workers), deserves attention and encouragement. Job splitting, at the outset, requires a more cautionary approach. Sharing work to create work is one thing; dividing jobs to create jobs may prove in reality to be very different. If work sharing is shared misery then the argument is reduced to 'anything is better than nothing'. Leaving aside the moral problems; socially, financially and psychologically, it may not.

Job sharing, in theory at least, has job creation potential. Job sharing schemes, if they are to succeed in the long term, have to demonstrate benefits to the individual moving from a full time job to half-a-job, to the employer operating the scheme and to the workforce as a whole. If they do not distinctly benefit both individual and employer their application will be strictly limited – witness the failure to get off the ground of the government's job-splitting scheme. If they are not accepted by the workforce as a whole, if they are just seen as changing full time to part time jobs, then again their chances of success appear small. The voluntary decision to share a job and its benefits is obviously different from an enforced switch to part time work with a loss of rights and benefits. The more job sharing resembles the latter rather than the former, the more likely it is to be an expedient rather than a solution and the more likely the scheme will fall into disrepute.

There are clear differences between job sharing in its fullest sense and job splitting.(25) The arguments have been well-rehearsed elsewhere and the failures of the United Kingdom's Job Splitting Scheme speaks for itself. The government has sought to amend its earlier provisions but deficiencies remain.(26) It offers a little to the previously unemployed 'sharer', not much to the employer, neither to the unemployed 'sharer' nor to his fellow workers. It does seek to directly affect unemployment but that seems to be its sole purpose.

Applications

Job sharing, in its fullest sense, may not be widely applicable nor might it prove to have any significant impact on unemployment. Equally, the potential for introducing job sharing may well be limited either to those on a high income, professionals in the main for whom half their previous salary is still a satisfactory income, or to those coming to the end of their working life where the demands made on their wage are not so great. A great deal of the literature in this area is directed at emphasising the potential for women to improve their lot within the world of work.(27) Publications by the Equal Opportunities Commission and New Ways to Work do not see job sharing mainly in terms of a solution to unemployment, indeed far from it, they see it as a way of offering employment opportunities to a group of people for whom previously such opportunities were limited i.e. women; and in particular married women with children: '... greater flexibility in working hours is perhaps the most important measure which could bring about an improvement in women's opportunities.'(28)

Job sharing has undoubtedly had its major impact, in its different guises, on female employment. Professional job sharers are predominantly, if not exclusively, female. Clerical job sharers, particularly in a number of the major banks, are again confined to women workers. At shopfloor level in manufacturing industry, the only schemes of any significance involve almost solely female employees. There are pros and cons to all these schemes: the lower down the scale one goes – from professional white collar workers, through white collar workers to blue collar workers – the more the pros diminish and the cons multiply, it would appear. However, the fundamental equating of job sharing with female employment remains. It would be a remarkable leap foward from the modest encouragement of job sharing which exists in certain quarters today to a situation, as advocated in a report to the Equal Opportunities Commission, in which: 'All jobs should be open to one full timer or 2 part timers and advertized as such.'(29) On consideration, it would probably be a remarkable leap backwards.

Job sharing, unlike moonlighting or additional employment, assumes that a person's primary source of income will come from half-a-job. It is an idea as yet anathema to the vast majority of the adult male population in this country, whether employed or unemployed. Education in the areas of sharing domestic responsibilities, the removal of sexual stereotyping of certain kinds of activity and employment into 'men's work' and 'women's work' and the use and enjoyment of leisure, has many light years to go before this fundamental fact is likely to be changed. Job sharing in its true sense has much to commend it but, short of compulsion, its impact upon unemployment is likely to primarily concern female job seekers and leave unmoved the bulk of male unemployed. Its attraction to the young male unemployed – the largest single group – can be expected to be minimal.

Trade unions tend to be confused by job sharing and distinctly wary of part time work. Employers favour part time work, particularly if they are seeking a predominantly female workforce, but seem reluctant to accept the case for job sharing as an alternative to part time work. There are small signs of progress being made in regard to attitudes on both counts but practical outcomes should not be assumed. The prospects of job sharing emerging from its status as surrogate part time work seem confined to a narrow band of professional occupations and these mainly (if not quite only) affecting women workers.

Accepting a narrow application, what has job sharing to offer? The answer, of course, entirely depends on how it is organized. At best it has a great deal to offer to the agreed sharers, plus advantages to the employer of guaranteed cover with minimal sickness and absenteeism.(30) In certain cases 'job sharing' can provide employers with increased labour flexibility, although some of these schemes are better viewed as a form of part time work than job sharing. One of the benefits of sharing a job should be shared leisure (the major reason why professional white collar workers seek to become job sharers). If leisure is limited or merely optional - as with 'job sharers' who have contractual hours of 39 or 40 a week (e.g at GEC Aycliffe) - the scheme's benefits in regard to flexibility are shifted from employee to employer. Ideally job sharing should strike a balance between the two.

Re-labelling part time work as job sharing is unlikely to provide a good advertizement for the product.(31) If to be a job sharer, as in certain instances, it is first of all necessary to be committed to a full time job then the scheme is more characteristic of work sharing than job sharing. Work can be shared and a greater number of individuals may earn some income (as well as having the potential of becoming full time workers) but the job sharing aspect is strictly limited. In the long term, if job sharing is to make an impact on changing working patterns, it has to be viewed as an option rather than an expedient. The element of choice seems fundamental to the concept. Although, for reasons of comprehension, the question of 'job sharing' was not posed in the JCF survey, it is clear that for many of the part time sample job sharing might well have proved a viable and desirable option as it could well have suited their need for choice and for restricted hours of working - like 'job sharers' very few part time workers appear to be seeking full time employment nor do they want to increase their hours that much. The element of flexibility in job sharing might well prove appealing to part time workers.

Developments

The distinction between job sharing and part time work must be recognized. Job sharing should be voluntary, it should involve dividing the contractual week in two and should, fundamentally, involve the sharing of all benefits i.e. not just wages and weekly hours but pensions, holidays, and other benefits. Equally it should not involve the loss of basic employment rights. Simply because pairs of part time workers enter into an agreement to provide cover for one another does not make it job sharing. 'Job-sharers', for example, at the Rolscreen Company, Iowa have a minimum contract of 1,000 hours a year but can work up to 40 hours a week. This is flexible part time working. It is stretching the point, disregarding the aspect of shared benefits and employment rights, to call an employment contract which provides for a working week of anything between 20 and 40 hours as job sharing.

Job sharers and part time workers do have one thing in common - they nearly all voluntarily choose reduced hours and are not interested in full time work as usually defined. However, the range of options available to those who wish to work something less than full time is extremely narrow. It is usually part time, 16 to 20 hours a week, or nothing. Some employers are beginning to widen choice. A Munich department store (Modehaus Beck) gives employees a choice of average monthly hours from 50 to 170. Sales assistants, who receive a commission on sales, have annual time contracts but they can choose when they work. Naturally most work at peak shopping times, when high sales are made, with far fewer working at slack periods. This sort of option might be particularly appropriate to retailing but the principle is capable of far wider application.

Those prepared to give up income for time may not be large, but when the usual option is full time or part time or, more often full time or no time, then demand becomes difficult to judge. In Britain when rationalization is threatened, it is usually a question of so-many full time jobs to go. The redundancy carrot is dangled and invariably (and it is not necessarily being argued unwisely) gobbled up. When a similar situation occurred to state employees in Santa Clara County, as a consequence of budgetary cut-backs, the trade unions negotiated a series of options:

1. keep current pay and hours
2. lose 5 per cent annual income and gain 10½ days holiday
3. lose 10 per cent annual income and gain 21 days holiday
4. lose 20 per cent annual income and gain 42 days holiday (to be taken in 2 separate 'blocks').

It is reported that nearly 20 per cent of the workforce voluntarily (though no doubt seeing the writing on the wall) requested one of the options (2) to (4) - most choosing (2) or (3). Is this a more constructive approach to threatened redundancies or lay-offs? Circumstances make cases but, leaving aside the question of adversity and duress, would it not be more socially beneficial if employers were encouraged to develop such time-income trade-offs? Do we all need to be working half time or full time and nothing in between?

V time

Voluntary reduced time initiatives are few and far between. In fact one of Britain's leading authorities on job sharing and new working patterns, Pamela Walton, recently stated that:

> 'as far as ... (we are) ... aware there are no overall schemes in Britain where employers allow their employees the opportunity to reduce their contractual hours of work with corresponding reduction in pay (V-time)'(32)

And yet job sharing is expanding, albeit on a modest scale, and the government is about to have a second stab at job-splitting. Why are there not more options between full time and part time work from which employees might choose? The answer usually lies in terms of regulation and control - uniform contracts covering large chunks of workforces being the order of the day rather than a range of individual contracts. However, the spread of female part time work, the growth of temporary work ('supplementary workers', as they are sometimes called), and the expansion of sub-contracting services, are all combining to erode traditional employment contracts. What is often missing from these developments is an adequate provision of choice from the point of view of the individual employee. Lacking choice, skills are often under used to the detriment of both employers and society in general.

Options

The provision of part time work to the unemployed through 'job sharing' schemes faces many difficulties. The creation of full time work by people in existing full time employment choosing, voluntarily, to job share has few difficulties. It is impossible to gauge how many people in full time employment would consider job sharing if encouraged to do so (e.g. by a personal subsidy or a government subsidy to the employer to promote job sharing and to cover training costs). From the JCF survey evidence it would appear that only 8 per cent of full time employees did not work full time out of choice. However, there is some evidence that trading income for leisure (or the opportunity to do other things which might even include earning additional income), whilst retaining secure job rights, might prove popular among certain age groups and categories of worker e.g. some 32 per cent of the full time employee sample would like or expect to work part time at some point in the future. The alternative of asking/coercing individuals to split their jobs with an unemployed person, and equally to ask the unemployed to accept that 'half-a-job-is-better-than-no-job-at-all', may offer work but unless it is an offer they cannot refuse (as has been suggested), does not offer a real job and does require a rare degree of individual self-sacrifice. The workforce which adopts a form of collective self-sacrifice, when it perceives little echo elsewhere, will indeed be an oasis in the desert.

The conditions under which job sharing is likely to succeed in a large organization will probably be peculiar to that organization alone. However, this is not to say that policy options do not exist for government. What is required is that government takes a longer term look at its job sharing initiatives. If the sole purpose is to take people off the unemployment register in order to improve the figures (or prevent them worsening more rapidly) then the concept will be lost to expediency. The result will not be job sharing but subsidized part time work. A more laudable objective would be the promotion of genuine job sharing in order to make room for the unemployed to move into full time jobs and thereby fostering a pattern of employment which could well prove socially and economically beneficial in the long run. As one observer recently commented:

> Job sharing may be seen as a true 'grass roots' movement, with little support and sometimes active opposition from unions and managements alike. Although conceived in large part to provide equality of opportunity for working women, job sharing has also been the object of scorn from certain feminist groups in Europe, who see job sharing as merely creating another women's ghetto in the labour market, and reinforcing the role of women in the home ... Despite conceptual and practical problems, however, wherever job sharing has managed to make an appearance it turns out to be a remarkably positive work/life solution for those involved. And that is the point to stress in conclusion ... it is a solution. It cannot meet the needs of everyone, or even of everyone who wants to work shorter hours, but it is one option that should at least be studied, to see if it should be made available for those who want it, because it can be highly successful and is evidently strongly desired by some ... 'evidently', because they have had to overcome such odds to achieve it. (33)

C Overtime

Comparative rates

Britain has consistently had some of the highest overtime rates in Western Europe, and is one of the few countries not to legislate against excessive working hours. The conversion of overtime hours into new jobs has been questioned and there is obviously no automatic translation as some simplistic analyses would have it.(34) It has been extrapolated that if overtime working were eliminated and the time spent on it redeployed, some one million plus new jobs could be created.(35) Unemployment has more than doubled since 1979 (by that year's definitions) but there is little evidence of a reduction in overtime working among male manual workers (where it is at its greatest). In fact the signs are that recent improvements in economic performance have been associated with increasing overtime (38) - see Table 6.14.

Table 6.14
Overtime (operatives in manufacturing industry)

Great Britain	Operatives (thousand)	Percentage of all operatives	Average hours per operative working overtime	Hours of overtime worked Actual (million)
1981	1,137	26.6	8.2	9.37
1982	1,198	29.8	8.3	9.93
1983	1,209	31.5	8.5	10.19
1984	1,297	34.3	8.9	11.39
1985	1,329	34.0	9.0	11.98
1986	1,304	34.2	9.0	11.72
1987	1,359	36.1	9.3	12.68

Comparative figures have shown Britain, as stated, to have high levels of overtime working.(37) It has also been argued that those countries which have adopted tighter controls on overtime working have been more successful in the past in lowering weekly hours. Although it has to be noted that the countries with 'tighter controls' - Austria, Belgium, Norway and Sweden - have much smaller workforces and the ability to regulate overtime may be that much easier.(38) Nevertheless, it is instructive to note that in Britain, trade unions in the engineering industry have sought to restrict overtime to 30 hours a month and more recently to 26 hours a month. Ignoring their lack of success in keeping to this formula, the question arises as to what kind of restriction it is which condones annual overtime of between 312 and 360 hours a year? In Austria that is over five times the legal limit (a country with low unemployment). A 'restriction' which allows for 6 hours of overtime a week for every person employed - and is then unenforceable - suggests either that the problem is not considered to be serious or that it is but that voluntary agreements are incapable of tackling the question.

In Britain, for all the hot air expended on the subject, the voluntary approach has proved to be totally unsuccessful in reducing overtime. Trade unions at national and local level have been either unable or unwilling to cut overtime working. The TUC has struggled to obtain a policy on overtime working but eight years of its 'Campaign for Reduced Working Time' has failed to develop either a coherent voluntary approach (no targets have ever been stipulated) or a detailed legislative alternative, although since 1986 it has been in favour of some form of legislative approach. This failure cannot be laid at the door of Congress House, but at the feet of the General Council and the major affiliated unions whose leaders have proved to be better speech-makers than policy makers on the subject.

It would be extremely naive to imagine that a legislative embargo on overtime would solve much of the unemployment problem. However, the question of excessive overtime working and the implications of its reduction on employment creation are matters for serious investigation. It is somewhat ironic to observe that the average amount of overtime per overtime worker today accounts for between 20 and 30 per cent of that person's annual wage. In April 1947, at the beginning of post-war reconstruction and at a time of 'full employment', the average amount of overtime worked per person accounted for less than 3 per cent of their annual wage.(39)

Time-off

Overtime is a thorny question. In certain cases it may arise as a consequence of skill shortages, more commonly it is a product of fluctuating demand.(40) Nevertheless, a lot of overtime is habitual, detrimental to job creation and indicative of economic inefficiency. Regular overtime breeds systematic overtime in order to maintain incomes. It has been argued that to effectively deal with excessive overtime requires a system where payment for extra hours worked came in the form of time-off in lieu. This would discourage the systematic use of overtime and would weaken employees' financial dependence on overtime working. The payment of additional working hours above a specified working week by commensurate blocks of leisure time is an interesting concept. It is one which has been largely neglected in Britain. The concept of gaining leisure as a result of extra hours worked has not been widely canvassed. Much of overtime working is weekend working. If time-off in lieu was provided for weekend working, leisure would be gained as payment in hours would have to be on a time-and-a-half or double-time basis. On the realistic assumption that overtime working may be limited but will always remain with us, the idea of trading work for leisure rather than income deserves attention. If there is potential for major employment creation through reduced overtime working, leisure trade-offs would appear to offer a practical way forward. Certainly an encouragement of the view that leisure should be seen as a positive reward from work is a healthier outlook than one which seeks to argue that leisure is somehow compensation for being unemployed. Leisure is only really meaningful if a person has the means to enjoy it.

Time-off in lieu, 'time bank' schemes and overtime reduction schemes have been developed in a number of instances:

* Massey Ferguson in Coventry operate a time bank scheme to bridge the gap between the contractual 39-hour week and a worked 40-hour week - time banked to be taken as extra holidays or to facilitate earlier retirement at full entitlement

* paid overtime has been eliminated at Petrofina by means of time credits on the basis of time-off in lieu as part of a productivity and flexibility package

* five-crew shiftworking has substantially reduced overtime worked at Fort Sterling paper making division, Wigan

* overtime payments have been abolished at Whitbread (Romsey, Hants) under a committed hours annual contract based on time-off in lieu.

Costs

It has been argued that the cost of overtime is relatively small compared to that of employing additional labour. However, this assumes that overtime working is as economically efficient as adequate cover and manning. There is evidence that excessive or high overtime creates problems of man-management and organization which contrive to raise unit costs. Overtime is often associated with high sickness and absenteeism rates. The impact on unit costs of reducing overtime to a minimum is not always appreciated by employers until changes are made e.g. by introducing new technology or new working patterns which affect overtime. Systematic overtime exemplifies both weak management and weak trade unionism and results in inefficient production. It is often easier to see overtime as a solution rather than altering working practices.(41) Equally, contrary to popular belief, overtime is often a consequence of over-manning rather than under-manning. 'Making work for the weekend' in order to get time-and-a-half and double-time does not represent efficient production. Neither does it make for efficient employment.

Industries in which workers are over-reliant on overtime working as an element of their weekly wage have been and will be in wage rate difficulties when new technology removes the need for much of that overtime.

Trade unions, it has been observed, are often unprepared and unable to tackle overtime as it forms an important element of many low paid workers incomes. However, it is a chicken and egg situation. Excessive overtime is most prevalent among those with low hourly rates and, whilst it helps to raise their incomes, it also ensures the retention of low hourly rates.(42) Low pay breeds overtime which in turn breeds low pay.

Britain in comparison with its major Western competitors, has traditionally had a low basic wage economy with a built-in ability in many industries to boost earnings through overtime. The consequence, however, has not been a net high wage economy. In fact, it has been a low-wage and long hours economy, despite the so-called 'strength' and 'power' of the British trade union movement. The 'productivity' problem, a favourite theme of economists, governments and their advisers during the 1960s and 1970s, was 'solved' - to a degree - by keeping wage rates down and paying large elements of earnings in productivity bonuses and overtime premia. Labour was cheap relative to capital and the consequence was a failure to make a radical re-assessment of working practices. The route to a high productivity/high wage economy - involving new technology, capital investment, work reorganization and flexible manning - was largely eschewed. Of course, many other factors were present which contributed to lack of economic success and, it is true to say, Britain has a peculiar fascination with labour problems and a remarkable propensity to lay economic ills at the door of employees and trade unions. However, it can be stated that too often low wages, low productivity and high overtime earnings (as a percentage of overall wage) were allowed to exist side-by-side. Overtime can be seen as just as much the cause of low wages as its product. Trade union and management reluctance to tackle overtime has done more to perpetuate low hourly rates and low pay than the achievement of productivity deals and bonuses has done to raise earnings.

Employment

The employment creation potential of a legislative attack on overtime working can too easily be exaggerated. Case study work has argued that the impact will not be as great as some of the predictions - often based on a crude translation of overtime hours into full time job equivalents - have suggested.(43) However, what is certain is that the pace of technological change in manufacturing industry is such that the continuation of systematic overtime can only tend to further redundancies. Tackling overtime ought to be viewed as much in the context of saving jobs as creating jobs. It makes little sense reducing contractual weekly hours if the major consequence is an increase in overtime working.

Opposition to legislative interventions regarding overtime (also to the shorter working week) is strong. It has been argued that overtime working is not detrimental to the economic success of companies. However, there are few sectors where systematic overtime has been demonstrated to be a source of economic efficiency. The case concerning individual companies' inefficiency through overtime working may not be entirely proven, but the evidence favouring it is greater than the obverse. Equally, some proponents of overtime have argued that it is not detrimental to the employment prospects of the unemployed.(44) This appears odd when the sectors and occupations where overtime is high are compared with the occupational requirements of the bulk of the unemployed. Overtime predominates among male manual workers as does unemployment. Is it suggested that the elimination of systematic overtime would have no beneficial job consequences?

Overtime restrictions

The social benefits of reducing systematic overtime have seldom been examined. It has been noted that the major hindrance to the development of employment opportunities for women is the redistribution of household work. Whether the reduction of regular weekend overtime working would help re-distribute housework is problematic. However, a wide range of individual benefits - including additional domestic responsibilities - have been found in case studies where new working patterns have helped to reduce overtime and provide 'longer leisure blocks'.

Even the most sceptical studies of the job creation potential of a crack-down on overtime are forced to conclude that the replacement of premium payments by time-off in lieu would have a significant impact on reducing overtime.(45) The means of changing cash payments to time payments have been explored in other countries. In certain cases there are premium payments for the first so many hours of overtime before switching to time-off in lieu; in the odd rare instance all overtime is paid by time-off.

It is a little difficult to argue, as Britain's laxity in regard to overtime working is almost unique among her European counterparts and major competitors, that restrictions on overtime would raise unit costs and impair productivity. Many case studies show the reverse to be true. Excessive overtime is indicative of bad management, poor trade unionism and slack working practices. The barriers to its removal are the conservatism of governments, employers and trade unions. To tackle weekly working hours without tackling overtime is a bit like buying a car on the basis of how old it is without bothering to check the mileage. It serves as much purpose parading a 38-hour week agreement knowing that annual working time is excessive and will remain unaffected, as it does showing-off a two-year old car in the knowledge that underneath the bonnet lies a clapped-out engine. Appearances are nice but they don't alter cases.

The reduction of overtime working by male manual workers ought to be a necessary adjunct to the harmonization of conditions between 'staff' and 'employees', blue collar and white collar workers. It is somewhat odd that in general manual hours in Europe tend to be below non-manual hours, whilst in Britain they are significantly higher. New technology, by blurring traditional distinctions between blue and white collar work, ought to precipitate the erosion of out-dated differential treatment between sections of the workforce. Holidays have largely been harmonized - why not annual working time?

The most effective means of tackling overtime is either solely through a legal annual overtime limit or by means of a legal annual limit combined with a system of time-off in lieu. The French have opted for an annual limit of 130 hours a year. Legislation to limit overtime to 100 hours a year per person and to be paid in time-off in lieu was proposed in Denmark but not enacted. In Belgium recent legislation has set upper limits of 65 hours of overtime per person per quarter to be paid at time-and-a-half with the 'half' being in cash and the 'time' being paid as time-off in lieu. Ireland has recently legislated for overtime limits of 40 hours a month or 100 hours a quarter. To be practical any legislation would have to be limited to workplaces employing over 100 people or companies employing over 1,000 people.(46) The monitoring of working time ought to be a joint responsibility of management and workforce representatives and could quite easily be appended to the statutory duties of health and safety representatives or joint consultative bodies. However, it remains unclear whether the legislative approach is desirable. It could be argued that it would ill-fit a doctrive of greater choice over personal working time.

All things being equal (which they never are), voluntary initiatives in the field of overtime reductions, particularly the payment of time-off in lieu, ought to be the desired goal. Some 66 per cent of the JCF sample wanted either no overtime (42 per cent) or very little (24 per cent in favour of 1 to 5 hours a week) if they had a free choice in the matter. Combined with a lack of interest in 'second jobs', it would suggest that the majority of people are not solely concerned with maximising earnings through long working hours. However, few want to lower their standards of living in return for more leisure. The problem with overtime is that people become dependent upon it in order to maintain a particular standard of living. Outside of compulsion there are few easy answers. A short term approach would be to seek to maximize the opportunities for adopting working patterns which seek to minimize the amount of overtime worked. It is to such schemes that the study will now turn.

Notes

1. O Robinson - The changing labour market: the phenomenon of part time employment in Britain, <u>National Westminster Bank Quarterly Review</u>, November 1985 pp 19-29.
2. See - J. Hurstfield - <u>The Part time Trap</u> (Low Pay Unit, London, 1978)
3. Some 59 per cent of part time workers are working mothers and a further 18 per cent are over retirement age
4. Institute of Manpower Studies, Manpower Commentary No. 18 - <u>Job Sharing</u> (IMS, University of Sussex, 1982) p. 19
5. M. Lucas - 'Le travail a temps partiel' (1979) quoted in Commission of the European Communities - <u>'Voluntary Part time Work'</u> (EEC, Brussels, 1980 - COM (80) 405 final) p. 7
6. This type of regulation would break EEC guidelines which stipulate that: 'Part time work must be voluntary and open to both men and women. It must not be imposed on persons who wish to work full time'. See EEC - 'Voluntary part time Work' <u>op. cit.</u>, p. 6
7. See F. Cairncross - 'Don't blame it on the chip' - <u>The Guardian</u> (17.10.83) p. 17

8. See EEC - 'Voluntary part time Work' op. cit.; EEC Draft Directive of Part time Workers Rights; Institute of Manpower Studies - 'Job Sharing' op. cit.; IMS - 'Worksharing Potential: An Examination of Selected Firms' (IMS, University of Sussex, 1981); and C. Leicester - Part Time Employment in Great Britain (EWCS, 1981)
9. See Employment Gazette, October 1982, pp. 411-12
10. See C. Leicester - 'Estimates of part time employment and the normal working year during the next 25 years', Institute of Manpower Studies, October 1977 (University of Sussex)
11. For a review of some of the arguments see D. Clutterbuck and R. Hill - The Remaking of Work (Grant McIntyre, London, 1981) pp. 39-73
12. As the IMS report on 'Worksharing' (op. cit. p. ii) states, 'the growth of part time working will occur without intervention.' It further argues '... pressures for an increase would be pushing on an open door', (op. cit. p. 16)
13. See, in addition to previous EEC references on part time work, 'A New Action Programme on the Promotion of Equal Opportunites for Women 1982-85' (EEC, Brussels, 1981 - COM (81) 758) and 'On the Reduction and Reorganization of Working Time' (EEC, Brussels, 1982 - COM (82) 809).
14. J.I. Gershuny - 'Who Works? Some Views of the Labour Supply' WASTE paper, May 1981, p. 23
15. See P. Willmott and M. Young - The Symmetrical Family. (Routledge and Kegan Paul, London, 1973)
16. See TUC Campaign for Reduced Working Time Progress Report, No.11 December 1983, p. 7
17. As R.E. Pahl has recently pointed out ('De-industrialization and social polarization' - first draft - mimeo, University of Kent, 1983) there is no incentive for the wife of an unemployed man to take a part time job (only 2 per cent of wives of unemployed men have part time work: L. Rimmer and J. Popay - Employment Trends and the Family, Study Commission on the Family, 1982, Table 7. Wives of unemployed husbands, who are active full time workers, would not be registered as unemployed even if they were seeking employment
18. A Department of Employment survey argued: 'There is little evidence that part time work has grown at the expense of full time employment'.
19. Although again, this will largely benefit households where the husband is employed and will do little to benefit the low-paid and worse off families. The case for subsidising this form of employment opportunity seems marginal to that of subsidising full time employment for families without work and heavily dependent on the benefits system
20. A useful statistical breakdown of part time working is to be found in 'Trends in Working Hours', Employment Gazette, November 1982 (pp. 477-486) pp. 478-481.
21. See, for example:
   A. Boyle - 'Job sharing: a study of the costs benefits and employment rights of job sharers' (New Ways to Work, London, November 1980)
   Equal Opportunities Commission - 'Job sharing: improving the quality and availability of part time work' (EOC, July 1981)
   Industrial Relations Review and Report - 'Two people, one job: an IRRR review of job sharing' No. 225, June 1980, pp. 5-9
   Industrial Relations Review and Report - 'Why split jobs?' IRRR, No. 287, 11th January 1983, pp. 2-8
   New Ways to Work 'Job sharing: an emerging work style'

International Labour Review, Vol. 118, June 1979, pp. 283-297
22. A caution not just peculiar to British unions. See J. Benson - 'Trade union attitudes to job sharing in Australia and some lessons for the U.K.' Industrial Relations Journal, Autumn 1982, Vol. 13 No. 3, pp. 13-19

23. See, for example, New Ways to Work - 'Job Sharing: A Guide for Employees' op. cit., pp. 2-4
24. For details of the original government scheme see Employment Gazette, August 1982, p. 323 and October 1982, p. 413
25. See, New Ways to Work - 'Job Sharing v Job Splitting' (London, 1983)
26. See 'Job-Splitting Changes', Employment News No. 109, July 1983, p.1
27. See particularly the Equal Opportunities Commission Report, op. cit., and A. Boyle, op. cit
28. Equal Opportunities Commission, op. cit 'Foreword'
29. A. Boyle, op. cit., p. 66
30. It has been argued that the savings through low absenteeism among job sharers alone provides a net financial benefit to the employer. See Euro-Fiet - 'Employment Creation and Working Time' (Brussels, 1982) p. 52
31. Particularly where it appears to breach EEC guidelines on part time work which state that: 'it must not be imposed on persons who wish to work full time', (Council of Ministers resolution 18.12.79). If all 'job sharers' must wish to work full time (and sign contracts of employment to that effect) and all employees are recruited part time, it would appear that they are automatically having something imposed upon them which they do not want
32. Work Times, Vol. 5 No.3 Spring 1987 p.3.
33. Joyce Epstein - 'Issues in Job Sharing' in New Forms of Work and Activity edited by R. Dahrendorf, E. Kohler and F. Piotet (European Foundation for the Improvement of Living and Working Conditions, Dublin, 1986), (pp. 39-88) P. 79.
34. A number of studies have shown figures for total overtime and 'full time job equivalents' - an example can be found in the House of Lords Select Committee Report on Unemployment, op. cit. p. 200
35. Labour Research Department - 'Overtime - the British Industrial Disease'. Labour Research, April 1980, pp. 78-79. The LRD do point out that this is a 'simplistic presentation'
36. See Employment Gazette July 1988, Chart 1.11 p. 517
37. See TUC Campaign for Reduced Working Time Progress Report No. 11 December 1983, p. 4
38. See Institute of Personnel Management - 'Work Sharing and Unemployment' (IPM, May 1983) p. 6
39. Despite cuts in the working week average weekly hours were longer in 1969 than they were in 1947. See National Board for Prices and Incomes Report No. 161 - Hours of Work, Overtime and Shiftworking (HMSO, London, 1970)
40. A review of some of the causes of overtime as well as its potential for work sharing based on case study work is to be found in the Institute of Manpower Studies Report - Worksharing Potential: An Examination of Selected Firms (IMS, University of Sussex, 1981)
41. The recent dispute over the proposed move to 6-day working in the coal mining industry at Margam in South Wales would have greater resonance from a trade union point of view if weekend maintenance working was not so widespread and systematically used throughout British coalfields
42. A recent extrapolation from New Earnings Survey data listed 17 top

overtime occupations and their average earnings as a percentage of the average manual wage. Only 1 out of 17 occupations would have had above average earnings if their overtime earnings were deducted. Some 5 of the 17 occupations actually had lower than average annual earnings even with their high overtime rates. See <u>Labour Research</u>, December 1983, p.320
43. See IMS study on 'Worksharing', <u>op.cit</u>
44. See, for example, M.K. Smith and S. Palmer - 'Getting to the Bottom of Overtime', <u>Personnel Management</u>, February 1981.
45. Even the Department of Employment has conceded as much. See 'Measures to alleviate unemployment in the medium term: work sharing', <u>op. cit.</u>
46. In manufacturing industry, some 80 per cent of all employees work in establishments employing over 100 people.

7 Working week or working life?

Working week preferences

In Chapter 5 it was suggested, from the JCF survey evidence, that the shorter working week was by no means as popular an option in regard to reduced working time as is often supposed. Longer holidays appeared to be preferred. In order to probe this further, an additional question was posed which included variations on the 'shorter working week' i.e. 4-day as opposed to 5-day working. The main findings are set out in Table 7.1.

Once again longer holidays were well-supported - favoured by nearly one-third of the sample - some 26 per cent of full time employees. However, the single most popular of the six choices was 'four-day working', even where this meant more hours per day. Some 35 per cent of the total sample chose this option - 39 per cent of the full time, 41 per cent of the male and 38 per cent of trade union members. The traditional approach, the preferred trade union approach, of shorter hours per day based on a five-day week, obtained nothing like the same support - 14 per cent of the total sample, 11 per cent of males and 11 per cent of trade union members. Although other variations can intrude - the shorter working week has often been negotiated on the basis of a short fifth day rather than minutes off each day - it did appear that the prospect of longer hours per day was outweighed for many by the prospect of 'longer leisure blocks'. The notion of a 'compressed work week' will be returned to again in Chapter 8, but the simple message appeared to be that different people in different circumstances might well make different choices were sufficient options available (it is perhaps of interest to note that in the occupational section the 4-day week obtained significant support in the following areas - 40 per cent of the manufacturing sample, 43 per cent of transport and construction, and 46 per cent of 'outdoor' workers).

The options discussed above do provide evidence that the thrust of the working time debate as perceived by its intended beneficiaries has been somewhat misplaced. For many people, extending the working day is not taboo if it generates greater leisure time. In trade union circles the 8-hour day is an historic milestone and one only to be broken at the pain of time-and-a-quarter, time-and-a-third, or time-and-a-half! The fact that the 8-hour day was originally achieved on the basis of six-day working appears to be ignored. However, whilst negotiations ought to consider the full range of options available, it is more likely than not that most discussion will still revolve around so many hours per week. This is particularly true at national or industry level where a 39 or 38-hour week will be negotiated and then left up to local circumstances to determine its implementation.

Accepting that major reductions will probably be of this nature, the sample were questioned in regard to a number of possibilities for the implementation of a 36-hour week. Key findings are set out in Table 7.2.

For full time employees, for whom such options would be a reality rather than hypothetical, as in the case of part time workers, the notion of a 4-day week proved the most popular single option - 37 per cent - followed closed by working a shorter fifth day - 34 per cent. Trade union members, perhaps surprisingly, favoured 4-day working to the shorter fifth day, more than did their non-union counterparts. Further, 4-day working proved particularly appealing to male workers - 41 per cent choosing it against only 24 per cent of the female sample.

The findings may be interpreted in a number of ways, but the least popular options for the sample at large and for full time employees was the notion of so many minutes off each day. This generated even less support than the notion of 12-hour working - a much more radical step for most employees. The appeal of 3-day or 4-day working was particularly strong in the 25-44 year old age range - over half of those in that range plumped for one of these two options: there was less enthusiasm for longer days among the oldest age-group, 55-64.

The attraction of shortening working hours by reducing the number of days worked whilst at the same time lengthening the working day, is not universal and it would be foolish to suggest that it was. Nevertheless, it is significant that two options which are rarely if ever posed to employees when shorter working time is mooted - those of 3 or 4-day working with longer hours - should be preferred by some 51 per cent of the full time sample, as opposed to only 45 per cent preferring the traditional approaches based on 5-day working!

<u>It would suggest that, depending on circumstances (occupation, nature of the industry/job etc.), significant sections of the working population would seriously consider lengthening the working day in order to achieve greater leisure time.</u> This survey data tends to be supported by case study evidence, mainly in process and manufacturing establishments, where - given the choice - employees have tended to vote with their feet for 'longer leisure blocks'. Trade unions at national level, however, remain opposed to such developments (although often turning a blind eye to local deals) even where there is evidence that lengthening the working day actually reduces annual working hours and cuts or eliminates systematic overtime. These matters will be further explored in Chapter 8, but at this stage some of the wider implications of the shorter working week, particularly its impact on employment, require consideration.

Table 7.1
Interest in ways of working less hours for same pay (Q15)

	Total	----------Age----------					Working		-----Sex-----		T.U. member	
		16-24	25-34	35-44	45-54	55-64	Full time	Part time	Male	Female	Yes	No
Total	523	97	142	135	110	39	414	109	308	215	206	317
Preference:												
5 day week - less hours per day	73 14%	20 21%	16 11%	19 14%	17 15%	1 3%	60 14%	13 12%	34 11%	39 18%	23 11%	50 16%
4 day working week - per day	184 35%	35 36%	55 39%	44 33%	36 33%	14 36%	160 39%	24 22%	126 41%	58 27%	78 38%	106 33%
Same hours - longer holiday	154 29%	30 31%	41 29%	35 26%	34 31%	14 36%	107 26%	47 43%	73 24%	81 38%	51 25%	103 32%
Longer period of education/training before starting work	10 2%	3 3%	2 1%	4 3%	1 1%	0 -	8 2%	2 2%	6 2%	4 2%	2 1%	8 3%
Sabbaticals	30 6%	4 4%	12 8%	11 8%	3 3%	0 -	25 6%	5 8%	20 6%	10 5%	12 6%	18 6%
Earlier retirement	53 10%	2 2%	11 8%	19 14%	14 13%	7 18%	45 11%	8 7%	38 12%	15 7%	31 15%	22 7%
Don't know/not sure	29 6%	3 3%	7 5%	8 6%	8 7%	3 8%	17 4%	12 11%	15 5%	14 7%	13 6%	16 5%

Table 7.2
Ways of working 36 hour week (Q16)

	Total	Age 16-24	25-34	35-44	45-54	55-64	Working Full time	Working Part time	T.U. member Yes	T.U. member No	Sex Male	Sex Female
Total	523	97	142	135	110	39	414	109	206	317	308	215
5 day week - shorter day	61 12%	10 10%	8 6%	26 19%	11 10%	6 15%	46 11%	15 14%	32 16%	29 9%	38 12%	23 11%
5 day week - shorter 5th day	183 35%	47 48%	49 35%	35 26%	35 32%	17 44%	140 34%	43 39%	65 32%	118 37%	89 29%	94 44%
Longer hours and fewer days (i.e. 4 day week and 9 hour day)	176 34%	28 29%	56 39%	43 32%	40 36%	9 23%	154 37%	22 20%	75 36%	101 32%	125 41%	51 24%
Longer hours and fewer days (i.e. 3 day week and 12 hour day)	71 14%	11 11%	21 15%	25 19%	11 10%	3 8%	56 14%	15 14%	29 14%	42 13%	44 14%	27 13%
Don't know/not sure	33 6%	1 1%	9 6%	6 4%	13 12%	4 10%	19 5%	14 13%	6 3%	27 9%	13 4%	20 9%

Shorter hours, employment and productivity

Britain has moved over the past 40 years from a standard 48 hour week to a standard 40 hour week, with a 39 hour week approaching fast. As Britain's workforce has expanded over the period, the shorter working week has obviously made a contribution to employment creation. Trade-offs between increased productivity and shorter working hours have occurred (particularly if one includes the growth of holiday entitlement over that period). This ought to be a salutary reminder to those who argue that shorter hours can only be bought by lower pay. Productivity improvements have consistently outstripped rises in real wages and there is little reason to believe that they will not continue to do so. The question ought to be not 'how' can we pay for shorter working time, but in what form - higher wages or lower hours - and in what proportion do we wish to be rewarded for rising productivity?

The impact of a radical reduction in the working week, unless accompanied by a series of other measures on employment creation, however, is more difficult to judge. The Department of Employment argued in 1978 that a move to a 35-hour week could reduce registered unemployment by between 100,000 and 500,000 (this at a time when unemployment 'only' stood at 1,400,000) depending on assumptions, but would increase labour costs by 6 to 8 per cent.(1) The increase in public expenditure, inflationary consequences and loss of competitiveness were considered to be too high a price to pay for the cut in unemployment. However, unemployment has doubled at least since 1978 and the working week has barely come down by 1 hour rather than 5. The arguments against reducing working hours will persist regardless of the economic situation. It is easier to argue the negative consequences of taking a particular action than the positive.

The shorter working week has spawned advocates and critics.(2) The specifics are not easy to judge. It could be a stimulus to increased productivity; it might, on the other hand, only result in overtime working. There could well be a problem of competitiveness if one country decided to go it alone on working hours, but it is difficult to argue this case from international comparisons. There is evidence of shorter working hours being introduced without increasing unit costs. However, the employment effects have been minimal.(3) The TUC itself has had to recently admit that the shorter working week has not proved job creative.(4)

Options and developments

Working hours will no doubt continue to fall in the long term, though in the short term there has been a slowing down process in recent years. The shorter working week will no doubt continue to be viewed as a major instrument of employment creation. However, whilst research into the implications of a reduction in the working week is plentiful in Britain at micro and macro-economic levels, very little attention appears to have been paid to the international ramifications of the shorter working week and there is little comparative analysis available of its costs and benefits. As the advocates of a shorter working week move closer and closer to a position of arguing for a legislative approach, better and more detailed international data would appear to be a priority. Equally, it is important that data regarding the standard working week is compared with the actual number of hours worked on an international basis. There is little point in legislating for a shorter working week if it has little or no impact on actual individual working time.

Taking one hour off the working week (normally on a Friday) has, quite obviously limited employment creation potential and, as the JCF survey shows, is little favoured by employees (see Table 7.1). The amalgamation of a shorter working week with 'flexi-time' arrangements could have greater potential. The need for additional cover or manning might arise if individuals use flexi-time to build up longer leisure blocks i.e. effectively working a longer working day than normal. The employment creation possibilities of flexi-time, as well as its impact on efficiency and productivity, are yet to be fully analyzed. However, as with most cases of reducing working time, it is not just the intent to reduce working hours which is important. The actual means of achieving it are the primary factor.

Trade unions, both nationally and internationally, have placed their main emphasis on reducing working time by cutting the standard working week (West Germany being a good recent example). The TUC's 'Campaign for Reduced Working Time', which argues the case for a 35-hour week, typifies this approach. It has been argued that a 35-hour week could yield up to half a million new jobs. However, these forecasts are dependent upon substantial improvements in productivity. If the shorter working week has a negative impact on productivity, then few if any new jobs will result.

In Britain there has been far less of a willingness to trade income for hours (such as in Belgium) or income for job security (such as 'concession bargaining' in the United States). Trade unions, probably reflecting the wishes of their members, have regarded the annual wage round as the battlefield of primary importance and, rheotrically, opposition to job losses a close second. However, there are few cases of redundancies being successfully opposed and very few (if any) cases of redundancies being combatted by some form of trade-off.

The TUC has demonstrated that it is prepared to discuss trading income for jobs.(5) The fact that trade unions have failed to link cuts in working time with job creation was underlined. However, the TUC can only encourage changes. It does not directly bargain with employers. That is the function of its affiliated organizations. Trade unions will continue to pay great attention to the shorter working week, but their success will have only a marginal impact on unemployment unless a more comprehensive bargain is struck on hours, conditions, income, overtime, unit costs and job security.

Legislation

To legislate across-the-board reductions in working time, as the French have done, causes many problems. For the average British worker the 39-hour week is a reality.(6) Many agreements have been signed providing lower basic hours (7) and there have been, in rare instances, the promises of a 35-hour week in parts of manufacturing industry.(8) Negotiating shorter basic hours does not appear to be impossible despite the CBI's claim to have 'stopped the rot' on hours.(9) What remains disturbing is that actual working hours show little sign of coming down - in fact are rising. There is no point in legislating across-the-board reductions in the working week without tackling annual working time and that means tackling overtime. Until trade unions are prepared to put overtime restrictions as high on their bargaining list as shorter working time then reduced hours will continue to have little effect on job creation. Equally, employers should be prepared to take a longer look at their employees average annual working time and its impact on sickness and absenteeism.

The shorter working week is not an end in itself. It is only a means to an end. If it is achieved without affecting annual working time, it will neither be a good thing for employment nor for productivity. It could provide a stimulus to both. However, to do so requires a further hard look at working practices. It is to be very much doubted that a serious examination of working practices would flow from the shorter working week unless it was linked directly to rewards - namely pay. This raises the question of trade-offs between time and productivity - an arena the recent negotiations between Engineering Employers Federation and trade unions (Confederation of Shipbuilding and Engineering Unions) sought to enter. The 37½ hour week was to be the reward for an agreement on 'flexible' working practices. Unfortunately, the talks collapsed but the principle remains - 'something for something' represents a better prospect of progress than the traditional 'nowt for owt' stance adopted by both sets of protagonists.

Holidays

The trend towards longer holidays in Europe is upwards. Four weeks is now common to most countries, in addition to statutory holidays. The 6-week annual holiday is a major target of European trade unions. The Department of Employment has estimated that an additional week of paid holiday could create 25,000 to 100,000 jobs but would raise labour costs by 2 per cent. In Britain there is no statutory minimum for annual leave. There is wide scope for bargaining holidays and a certain degree of success can be claimed with most workers (86 per cent) now enjoying over 20 days annual leave per year (see table 5.17 for detailed figures). Annual holidays have risen in piecemeal fashion and no doubt will continue to do so. As a conscious attempt at work redistribution, more radical initiatives to exchange income for holiday entitlements appear remote, although progress towards 5-weeks and, more slowly, 6-weeks annual entitlement can be expected. There may also be moves towards greater service-related holidays, perhaps in the form of sabbaticals. Further, there is some recent evidence to suggest that holidays may be a more favoured route to reduced working time. An IRS survey of the 1985/86 pay round showed that whilst only 6 per cent of agreements monitored included a cut in basic working hours, some 22 per cent raised basic annual holiday entitlement (IRRR, 22 October 1985).

The JCF survey data clearly points to employee preferences for longer holidays, (see Tables 5.18 and 7.1), particularly if solely a matter of choice between holidays and shorter hours per week. Even where the choice was widened to embrace a total of six options, longer holidays remained the first preference of some 29 per cent of the total sample. Perhaps significantly, some 43 per cent of part time employees favoured it as their first choice - probably reflecting poorer conditions of employment than their full time counterparts. The drive for reduced hours will need to embrace the wider context of the working year in which holiday entitlements will inevitably play a key role. Widening the debate further, the question of sabbaticals may also be an agenda item for the future.

Sabbaticals

Sabbaticals (leave of absence for a year or other periods at intervals in the work-cycle) can only be seriously considered if they are linked to education or training (even retraining) - otherwise people, in all probability, would simply drop into the informal economy for the duration of their leave. This would require a commitment to further adult education and training much greater than at present. The cost of sabbaticals would also need to be offset by government through changes to the tax/benefit system.

A practical approach to the extension of the principle of sabbaticals would appear to be short term sabbaticals based on the extension of service holidays i.e. holidays paid for by the employer on the basis of an employee's length of service. Entitlement to extra holidays for service is a common practice in other countries and has expanded during the 1970s in Britain. The stipulation, for example, of an additional two weeks' leave every seventh year of a person's service would minimize the impact on unit costs and would give the individual employee suitable longer blocks of leisure time to enjoy as retirement approached.

Age	(e.g. person joins a company at 16) Extra service blocks additional to normal holidays
23 =	+ 2 weeks
30 =	+ 4 weeks
37 =	+ 6 weeks
44 =	+ 8 weeks
51 =	+ 10 weeks
58 =	+ 12 weeks
65 =	+ 14 weeks

Even if a person worked 50 years for a single employer, their additional service holidays would only amount to a maximum 56 weeks during a working lifetime. However, the concept of some form of 'sabbatical' would have been established and would be seen to be directly linked to concepts such as 'loyalty' and 'commitment' to the company, popular themes in industrial relations these days.

The 'older' the age profile of a company's workforce, the greater cover it would need to employ to compensate for such 'sabbaticals'. The amount of extra holidays/leisure afforded for service could be greater or less, as could the gaps between the awards. However, the options for 'staged' or 'flexible' service-holidays appear greater than those of fixed annual sabbaticals.

There are valid criticisms of service holidays. They might encourage employers to replace older workers and they could also discourage job mobility. However, pension rights are probably a greater discouragement to job mobility than a block of holidays every seven years, and a minor incentive to companies to ensure a more 'balanced' age-profile of their workforce may be no bad thing, particularly for the young unemployed.

The JCF survey posed 'sabbaticals' as one of its six options in regard to working less hours for the same pay. Some 6 per cent of the sample named it in preference to other more obvious and commonly quoted methods - 15 per cent of the degree level sample. This would suggest that the concept is not entirely without support and, where other factors may intrude e.g. perceived levels of stress or where sense of company identity is strong, it may emerge from the cloistered groves of academe (soon to lose tenure) to affect other sectors of the working population.

Notes

1. See 'Measures to alleviate unemployment in the medium term: work sharing', Employment Gazette, April 1979, (pp. 400-402) p. 401.
2. See Treasury Working Paper No. 14 - R. Allen - 'The Economic Effects of a Shorter Working Week', London, June 1980.
3. See M. White - Case Studies of Shorter Working Time, Policy Studies Institute, No. 597 (PSI, London, October 1981).
4. See TUC - Campaign for Reduced Working Time, Progress Report No.9, (TUC, London, January 1983).
5. See 'Jobs not big pay rises line by TUC' - The Guardian (4.2.84) p. 3.
6. It has been estimated that 60 per cent of the 11 million manual workers covered by national agreements had basic hours of work of less than 40 per week - see Incomes Data Services, IDS Study, No. 300, October 1983 - 'Hours and Holidays' p. 2. The 'normal working week' for manual workers in all industries and services for 1983 was 39.3 (it was 40.0 in 1975 when unemployment was below 1 million: the actual working hours of full time men over 21 stood at 43.6 per week in 1975, by 1983 this had dropped - just - to 43.3 per week).
7. See, for example, 'Shorter Working Week Arrangements', Industrial Relations Review and Report', IR-RR 287, 11th January, 1983, pp. 9-14.
8. For example, Metal Box have signed a 35-hour week for its shopfloor employees who will primarily be working a continuous 5-crew, 12-hour shift system (produces a total of 142 - 143 shifts per person per year).
9. For a recent examination and analysis of negotiated reductions at national level see M. White - 'Shorter Working Time through National Industry Agreements', Department of Employment Research Paper No. 38, London, September 1982.

8 Developing approaches to annual hours

A Flexi-time

Trade union attitudes towards flexi-time were noted in Chapter 3. As stated, flexi-time has tended to be the preserve of predominantly white-collar office workers. In such areas the power of the 8-hour day would not seem to have so strong a hold, perhaps because for many office workers a 'normal' working day is around 7 hours and lengthening it may not pose such a problem.

The JCF survey asked for opinions in regard to flexi-time following an explanation of what the concept normally involved (see question 18 in questionnaire). A somewhat surprisingly high percentage of the sample – 23 per cent – claimed to work under some kind of 'flexi-time' arrangement (highest percentages were recorded among 'office worker' – 36 per cent – and those employed in 'services' – 30 per cent) – see Table 8.1.

For those who didn't work 'flexi-time', considerable interest in it as an option appeared to be present – see Table 8.2. That interest was particularly prevalent among the young (62 per cent of all 16-24 year olds) and females (55 per cent) members of the sample and among those employed in offices (62 per cent). The regulation of flexi-time and its adaption to the needs of a business or organization appear its main stumbling blocks. Nevertheless, it appears to be widely used and popular. It has often been assumed that 'harmonization' of terms and conditions between 'blue-collar' and 'white-collar' workers and between 'employees' and 'staff' would inevitably lead to the elimination of clocking procedures. The flexi-time movement may reverse this process. Equality in the future might require everybody to be time-recorded, and why not?

Table 8.1
Opinion of flexi-time (Q18A/B)

	Total	16-24	25-34	Age 35-44	45-54	55-64	Full-time	Part-time
Total currently have flexi-time	523	97	142	135	110	39	414	109
Yes	120 23%	18 19%	37 26%	26 19%	31 28%	8 21%	101 24%	19 17%
No	398 76%	78 80%	105 74%	108 80%	76 69%	31 79%	308 74%	90 83%
Dk/not sure	5 1%	1 1%	0 —	1 1%	3 3%	0 —	5 1%	0 —

Table 8.2
Whether would like to have flexi-time
(Base all do not have flexi-time)

	Total	16-24	25-34	Age 35-44	45-54	55-64
All answering	403 77%	79 81%	105 74%	109 81%	79 72%	31 79%
Yes	195 48%	49 62%	49 47%	51 47%	36 46%	10 32%
No	117 29%	20 25%	29 28%	34 31%	19 24%	15 48%
Dk/not sure	33 8%	4 5%	11 10%	8 7%	9 11%	1 3%
Not applicable to my job	58 14%	6 8%	16 15%	16 15%	15 19%	5 16%

B Shiftwork innovations

Five-crew shiftworking

Many of the advocates of reduced working time are unwilling to recommend shiftwork innovations due to a deep-seated dislike of shiftworking itself. However, where shiftworking exists, its extension, particularly by means of an additional crew on continuous production processes, can be both profitable to the employer and employment creative. The belief that more people to cover the same hours must be more expensive has not always proved to be the case. The impetus to change shiftwork patterns is often brought about by an expansion of production, problems of cover and overtime associated with the old system or the introduction of new technology. In all these cases opportunities exist to redistribute work. The range of options available in terms of working patterns are almost infinite.

Shiftwork innovations are not a live issue of any major dimension in Britain.(1) However, some employers who operate shiftwork systems are looking to more efficient manning levels and levels of cover. Equally many shiftworkers are looking to longer leisure blocks to help compensate for unsocial hours. The introduction of 5-crew shiftworking appears to offer the possibility of meeting both requirements.

On any continuous production system there are 168 hours a week to be covered (7 x 24). The usual response has been to base operations on a 4-crew system (4 crews working 42 hours a week = 168) as it matches more closely the contractual obligation of the 40-hour week (with the 39-hour week becoming more typical or even less). Most continuous production systems are augmented by other variations - groups of day-workers, double-day workers etc. - but the 'core' group of shiftworkers typically operates on a 4-crew basis. The obvious consequence of such a system is that there is at least 2-hours' overtime a week inherently built into it (the gap between the 42-hours worked and the 40-hours contracted), which is usually compensated by the provision of one lieu day a month (often worked as overtime), and no provision is made for statutory and contractual holidays. Sickness and absence also conspire to push up overtime levels. The regulation of 4-crew working varies and it would be wrong to exaggerate the impact of the system itself on overtime levels e.g. many continuous production systems incorporate periodic 'shutdowns' when holidays are taken. However, as contractual hours fall from 40 to 39 to 38 to 37, so the system becomes increasingly unwieldy - involving elaborate 'owed hours' arrangements, lieu days and problems of cover. In theory, 5-crew working offers a more viable solution.

A 5-crew system produces a theoretical 33.6 hour week (168 ÷ 5). This almost certainly means that the individual owes the company hours. Thus, holidays can be more easily accommodated and cover better arranged. Equally, as at American Can, maintenance shifts can be incorporated without the need for premium payments. The longer blocks of leisure time between shifts has reduced sickness and absence levels in certain cases. 5-crew working eliminates systematic overtime, usually provides 'leeway' in terms of contractual hours for the company to utilize as it wishes, allows for further reductions in the working week to occur without major dislocation and - by cutting annual working time - should lower sickness and absenteeism rates. Its disadvantages are mainly concerned with a certain amount of the necessarily staged summer holidays falling outside of school holidays - the holiday 'band' being widened from 8 weeks to 10 weeks (school holidays usually amounting to 6 weeks). The problem, of course, would be solved if there was a little more 'flexibility' to the annual holidays of school teachers. Does the curriculum require all of them to be off for the same 6 weeks every year? Are examination timetables set in tablets of stone? Could there not be a 'core' of 2 weeks within a 12 week spread (say July, August and September) and the remaining 10 weeks timetabled and weighted to allow sufficient cover but also to provide parents with a degree of choice? The growth of continental holidays, 'winter breaks' and the rise in individual annual holiday entitlements surely demands some consideration along the above lines; although, given current difficulties over teachers contractual hours and duties, it might not be an entirely propitious time to raise the issue.

5-crew working inevitably requires an additional 25 per cent to total manning levels provided that manning levels per shift are maintained. The potential increase in labour costs appears to be the major stumbling block to its wider implementation. However, the removal of premia payments for systematic overtime, improved working practices, the alteration of manning arrangements to allow for planned maintenance, reduction in absenteeism and sickness by the provision of longer leisure blocks and increased flexibility, can all combine to lower rather than raise unit costs. The outcome may be slightly higher labour costs but equally - if the change is used to reorganize work - it can prove to be more efficient and productive in the long term.(2) In the case studies of 5-crew shiftworking, now quite plentiful, there is no example of manning levels being raised by 25 per cent. The move to 5-crew shiftworking is usually associated with some kind of productivity deal e.g. American Can, ICI and Michelin.

Evidence for the job creation potential of the extension of shiftwork or the introduction of new shiftwork patterns is sketchy. However, the move to 5-crew working can only be beneficial in terms of employment. At present the economic benefits of such a move are being drowned by an emphasis on its potential social benefits. The two are not necessarily incompatible. Shiftworking innovations can be both cost-effective and employment creative. A problem for trade unions and employees, however, is that new jobs might be bought at the expense of the workers' incomes through a marked reduction in overtime earnings. The transition from a low wage/high overtime set-up to an enterprise based on high wages and low overtime will no doubt not be smooth everywhere. However, new technology does provide the opportunity for such a transition - if employers and trade unions have the foresight to seize it.

Longer shifts and the compressed work week

Reducing overtime and shortening the working week can largely be seen as traditional responses to the jobs crisis. Those in work should do a little (or a lot) less of it. Work redistribution and job sharing schemes take this reallocation of labour argument to its logical conclusion. However, it has been argued that a far more effective method of creating jobs is by radically changing patterns of working time, which may or may not require shorter contractual working hours. The provision of longer holidays and, perhaps more importantly, longer blocks of leisure time have been seen as means towards this end - 5-crew working being but one example of the latter.

Redistributing work to alter patterns of working time without necessarily changing contractual working hours has the advantage of being potentially cost effective. Employers who have experimented with new patterns of working time have done so precisely because it was cost effective. The argument that either costs or overtime would be raised no longer holds.(3) Trade unions have been reluctant to encourage innovations in working time which disturb historical bargaining gains - the 'Holy Trinity' of the 8-hour day, time-and-a-half for Saturdays and double-time on a Sunday. Nevertheless employees have often shown themselves eager to respond to initiatives which offer longer blocks of leisure time.(4)

The range of options available to companies or organizations considering new patterns of working time is formidably large.(5) The extent to which many of these options should be encouraged is perhaps more questionable.(6) However, it does seem perverse that an organization which introduces 10 or 12 hour shifts provides longer blocks of leisure time and effectively eliminates overtime working, can stand condemned; when long hours at overtime rates (i.e. over the 8 hours) is considered acceptable and when habitual Saturday and Sunday overtime working is for many employees a way of life. The JCF survey indicated that 13 per cent of full time employees worked every weekend, a further 21 per cent worked 'most weekends' and another 35 per cent worked 'occasional' weekends. Only 15 per cent of the sample were categorized as 'shiftworkers'.

Longer leisure blocks encompass a wide variety of practices - longer holidays, sabbaticals, the compressed or 4-day working week and shiftwork innovations (10 and 12 hour shifts and 5-crew working). They need not be associated with an overall reduction in contractual working time. However, their employment creation potential is arguably far greater than many schemes which seek an immediate cut in working hours. How work is organized is a powerful factor in the jobs/hours equation.

There may be, although the evidence is very patchy (there has not been an authoritative study on shiftworking in the UK since 1970), a trend towards the introduction of longer shifts i.e. 10 hour and 12 hour shift systems. These provide longer leisure blocks and can reduce overtime levels:

- 10-hour day or 10-hour shifts can be worked - usually on a 4 x 10 system. Thus the working week is reduced from five days to four days a week.(7)

- 12-hour days or 12-hour shifts lengthen the working day even further but reduce the working week to 3 or 3½ days or provide longer leisure blocks within a shiftwork system.

A recent agreement struck by the TGWU at a London engineering company (Winn and Coales) provides for a 4-day 35-hour week. The chief engineer is reported as saying that, 'We can run four longer days more efficiently' (Financial Times Times 9.10.85). However, it does break the eight-hour day and in many areas such an arrangement would not have received union endorsement. The movement towards 12-hour operations has met with union opposition, despite often providing much longer leisure blocks e.g. NEK cables agreement on 12-hour shifts which is based on only 140 shifts a year (an average of three per contractual week). It is suggested that the movement to 6-day working at the new Margam colliery will be accompanied by miners having one week off in five to compensate for Saturday working. In other industries, particularly on continuous production systems which already involve weekend working, the notion of longer leisure blocks has proved attractive to employees even though it has been achieved at the cost of lengthening the working day - a ballot at Esso Fawley offered four alternative systems, two based on 8-hour and two on a 12-hour working, with a 5-crew 12-hour system

111

receiving majority support.

The case study data mentioned could be said to have been supplemented and supported by the survey evidence discussed in Chapter 7. Longer shifts do appear to have an appeal where they 'compress' the working week down to 3 or 4 days. Only recently some 2000 employees at Land Rover's plant in Solihull have been recorded as operating a 4 by 9 hour shift pattern. The instances of 12-hour working are also multiplying. Where total annual hours are reduced and where health and safety issues are fully explored, there seems little reason to doubt that the examples of 3 and 4-day working will not continue to spread.

Weekend working

As working time is reduced and the working week becomes more compressed to 4½ days and 4 days, there would appear to be more rather than less pressure to work weekends. About 45 per cent of the working population work regularly on weekends (although not every weekend) and 1-in-4 work Sundays according to the Department of Employment. In comparison only 30 per cent of the JCF sample claimed 'never' to work weekends - see Table 8.3.

Table 8.3
Weekend working

LFS estimates
Great Britain, Spring 1986

Persons aged 16 and over in employment   Thousands

	Number	Per cent
All persons in employment*	23,830	100.0
Working weekends** of which:	10,697	44.9
Saturdays but not Sundays	5,006	21.0
Sundays but not Saturdays	766	3.2
both Saturdays and Sundays	4,905	20.6
Not working weekends	12,938	54.3

* Includes 196 thousand who either gave no reply when asked whether they worked weekends or were not asked whether they worked weekends as they were on government employent and training schemes and said they did no paid work in the reference week.

** Persons who worked on any weekend in the four weeks ending with the survey reference week. Includes 21,000 who said they had worked at weekends but did not state whether they worked on Saturdays, Sundays or both.

The number of people who work only at weekends is as yet unrecorded. However, there are examples of weekend-only shift operations being introduced, particularly where there is opposition from the existing workforce to move to continuous production. Weekend working can be introduced which effectively reduces the working week to 2/3 days or 2/3 shifts. In France a number of companies have augmented their continuous production systems with weekend working. In some cases less than a full week's wage is earned (e.g. 28 hours), whilst in others a standard 36 hour week is rewarded (although actual working hours are less).

As countries move closer to a 24-hour economy and as services are extended to cover weekends e.g. banking and retailing (currently limited by the Sunday trading hours), so the possibility of purely weekend working becomes more feasible. The need to utilize expensive capital equipment and computer technology only serves to strengthen this process. Traditional resistance to weekend working among those working during the week (despite its prevalence) has less force when people are being employed on contracts which provide for 4 to 5 days off per week.

C Annual hours contracts/annual time commitments

Shiftwork systems are inevitably based on some form of annual hours contract - the more complicated the shiftwork pattern the more an understanding of annual hours is required. Holidays are calculated on an annual basis as are most service requirements and entitlements. The pressure to move towards a greater incorporation of annual time notions rather than fixed weekly hours would appear to be inevitable despite the previously mentioned conservatism of approach from both sides at the bargaining table.

Annual hours systems in the more formal sense appear to be on the increase. A recent survey by the Industrial Society quotes 49 companies with such arrangements.(8) Some of the benefits listed are included in Table 8.4.

Table 8.4
Benefits of annualized hours

	Per cent
Reduced unit costs	33
Reduced overtime	33
Reduced absence	16
Labour flexibility	24
Increased productivity	22
Changed holiday arrangements	24
Employee benefits	10
Return to profitability	4

Source: Industrial Society

Examples include:
- Thames Board reduced hours from 41 to 39 per week on the basis of annualized hours and radically cut overtime working
- Norsk Hydro (Immingham) introduced an annual hours system as part of a rationalization programme which reduced contractual hours to 1600 a year and paid for overtime by time-off in lieu
- Ever Ready at Wolverhampton brought in an annual hours scheme to offset seasonal fluctuations in demand and cut the working week from 39 to 36 on a rearranged basis:

    - 25½ hours - January/February (3 days)
    - 34 hours - March/April   (4 days)
    - 39 hours - May/June   (4½ days)
    - 45 hours - July/November   (5 days)
    - mixed pattern during December

- Whitbread Romsey brought in a complex committed hours scheme in order to better match hours worked with workload and eliminate overtime
- Other examples include tanker drivers at Shell and Esso, BP Chemicals (Grangemouth) and BCL Cellophane (Barrow).

The key to the successful operation of annual time contracts is self-regulation. Like job-sharing they require that the necessary cover is provided. However, unlike most job-sharing schemes they should provide greater flexibility among groups of workers. There are problems associated with sickness but these are no different from more rigid systems. The emphasis should be on choice and collective agreement as to how particular groups of workers can cover the 'job'. Greater opportunities for annual time contracts exist where production is continuous but - as flexi-time has demonstrated - this need not necessarily be the case. There is, of course, greater emphasis on participation, group-work, self-supervision and self-organization.

'Annual time contracts' ought to stimulate the movement to an 'annual wage' rather than a system of hourly earnings (although checks and balances need to be built into any system until it is seen to work effectively) and also assist the harmonization of conditions. 'Staff' and 'worker' status are outmoded concepts. The only differential should be a wage differential. 'Annual time contracts' and 'flexi-time' arrangements should assist the equalization of employment conditions between blue collar and white collar workers.

Notes

1. Institute of Manpower Studies - <u>Worksharing Potential: An examination of selected firms</u> (IMS, University of Sussex, 1981) p.15
2. In some cases management have looked to more flexible working hours schemes in order to regain control over an inefficient and failing time system. See R.A. Lee - 'Recent trends in the managerial use of flexible working hours' <u>Personnel Review</u>, Vol. 9 No. 3 Summer 1980.
3. Although this does not necessarily mean that employment will be created either. Most shorter working week deals have been struck on a 'no rise in unit costs' basis.
4. Where resistance to flexible working initiatives has occurred, e.g. the train drivers initial rejection of and opposition to 'flexible rostering' (providing a 7 to 9 hour day instead of a fixed 8-hour day), it could be argued that it was partly a consequence of a failure of the initiative to provide meaningful longer blocks of leisure time. A driver had to average 39 hours a week when the longest day he could work was 9 hours. The workforce, unlike those who operate 'flexi-time'systems, had no control over the system of 'flexible rostering'. For a wider discussion of this issue see Bob Lee - 'Hours of work - who controls and how?' <u>Industrial Relations Journal</u> Vol. 14 No. 4 Winter 1983, pp. 70-75.
5. For a good introduction to some of these options see W. McEwan Young and S.J. Baum - A practical guide to flexible working hours (Kogan Page, London 1973) and Incomes Data Services - <u>'Guide to shiftwork'</u>(IDS, London, 1979).
6. For example, for a fuller discussion of the health and social aspects of both shiftworking and specific forms of shiftworking see: J.M. Harrington - <u>Shift Work and Health: a Critical Review of the Literature</u> (HMSO, London, 1978).

NEDO - F. Fishwick - <u>The Introduction and extension of shiftworking</u> (NEDO, London, 1980) J. Walker - <u>The Human Aspects of Shiftwork</u> (Institute of Personnel Management, London, 1978).

7. A system of working which has strong precedents going back twenty years in the United States. See R. Poor (ed) - <u>4 days, 40 Hours</u> (Pan, London, 1972).

8. G. Desmons and T. Vidall-Hall (1987) - <u>Annual Hours</u> (Industrial Society, New Series No. 6, London)

9 Conclusions

Working time ought to be about time worked, not time spent at work. Part of the argument in favour of reduced working time is based on the premise that too often long hours equal poor utilization. The aim should be to utilize working hours effectively, not perpetuate systems which reward people on their ability to remain locked within a building for the greatest length of time. However, critics might argue that shorter hours do not necessarily imply better labour utilization and that payment by time systems at best have an appearance of 'fairness' which more subjective reward systems do not possess. These arguments are valid - in industrial relations the perception of 'fairness' is fundamental to the wage/labour contract. Thus, this report is not arguing for the abandonment of time systems. On the contrary, it seeks to reinforce notions of payment - for time, but within a wider context than that which currently prevails - a context which seeks to match individual employee preferences with organizational needs on the basis of collective agreement.

Working time is being reduced despite the lengthening of weekly hours worked. Charles Hardy's 50,000 hour a lifetime worker - 32 hours a week for 45 weeks for 35 years - is a reality for some and a not too distant prospect for many. This effectively halves the working lifetime of the traditional 100,000 hnour a lifetime employee - 45 hours a week for 47 weeks for 47 years. Nevertheless many work long hours whilst others work none at all.

Working time options

The main theme of this report has been the reduction of working time and its potential redistribution as a result of the development of great personal choice and options in regard to working hours. Despite economic problems, an ageing workforce and a drop in the number of school leavers in the 1990s suggest that we ought to be encouraging entry into the labour market and not driving people out of it. The more of the working population which is employed the better. Work should be a practical choice for all. One of the barriers to be broken down in order to achieve the work-for-all option is that of working time. Rigidities need to be removed and choices opened up. The wider the distribution of work, the more choice and options will become available.

There are times in everybody's life when time is of more value than income. In Britain, for the most part, the only way to gain time is to be off work altogether and thereby sacrifice income, or jeopardize work by going 'on the sick'. This seems not only archaic but positively inefficient. In Sweden options are being developed for parents of young children to move from full time work to a six-hour day. Loss of income may arise but might be considered justified. On the other hand, it could enable both parents to retain full time jobs and provide greater income than might otherwise have been the case if one parent was forced to give up work. Flexible and phased retirement schemes have also recognized that there are workers at the other end of the working life spectrum who might appreciate wider options in regard to reduced hours.

Within a job sharing/part time working/reduced working time framework many options exist. The key elements suggested are:

1 the schemes should be voluntary and should form part of a properly formulated and detailed programme which is seen as ongoing and not the product of short term expediency.

2 reduced or new patterns of working time ought to be collectively agreed and contractually incorporated with the provision of equal employment rights to those pertaining for full time workers (benefits will, no doubt, be pro-rata)

3 procedures for moving between options - such as returning to full time employment or moving onto shorter hours - need to be specified and jointly (management and employee representatives) monitored and administered

4 the widest possible range of time-income and working time/leisure time trade-offs ought to be provided, even at the expense of lengthening the working day

5 the state ought to encourage trade-offs and schemes which have a direct bearing on the reduction of the registered unemployed.

Providing more flexible time-schedules is a bit like bathing in the sea - getting into the water is the hardest part. Companies and organizations who have dipped their toes into 'annual hours' or 'flexi-time' schemes have seldom floundered.

Voluntary vs negotiated hours reductions

The arguments for greater choice and more attention to employee preferences have been rehearsed throughout this report. Nevertheless, it is necessary to conclude that 'voluntarism' has its limits and what is being advocated is a reduction of hours by means of a collectively bargained agreement between employers and their workforces or group of workers and <u>not</u> individual time contracts

In the working time debate, distinctions are often made between <u>voluntary</u> (primarily as individual choice) and <u>negotiated</u> (collectively bargained) reductions. These distinctions may be false - voluntary schemes usually need to be negotiated and are sought for large sections, if not all, of a workforce. Nevertheless, voluntary schemes are usually seen as enabling agreements - options to be taken up or ignored as desired - whilst collective bargaining invariably seeks to achieve a universal reduction (such as an hour off the working week or extra holidays) applicable to all and enforceable on all. If free rein were given to the voluntary approach, a multiplicity of arrangements might apply across a particular workforce, whilst collective bargaining would seek to avoid too many deviations from the regulated norm. In many ways voluntary reduced working time poses a threat to collective bargaining as, taken to a logical conclusion, it seeks a variety of different individual arrangements as opposed to a collective agreement covering all. The trick is to ally the strength of the collective provision with the divergent individual preferences of the employees or groups of workers in question.

Most people desire a reduction in their hours of work - all things being equal. However, the point about working time is that all things <u>never</u> are equal. Ugly factors like income and standard of living intrude to upset the equation. There is a clear gap between a desire for reduced hours and the acceptance of a cut in income or standard of living in order to achieve it. The British survey evidence on this point was overwhelming. Thus, it is one thing to desire shorter hours on the same income, but quite another to accept that a reduction in income will be the price to be paid for increased leisure.

Equally, we find that those who would want reduced hours if their income remained the same, differ in regard to the kind of reduction they want and their preferences at different times of their working lives. Some would prefer a shorter working week, some more holidays and others a lowered retirement age (particularly the older they get). This is hardly surprising. Nevertheless, it is not always fully thought through by the apostles of shorter hours. There are assumptions made about the kind of reductions people would want with little attempt made to explore their preferences or the kind of options they might like in particular circumstances.

Voluntary reduced working time seeks to allow employees greater freedom in making decisions about the kind of hours they wish to work. It could cut across traditional negotiations, as has been suggested, but perhaps more importantly it raises the question as to whether or not the approach is desirable in itself. There are potential dangers:

1. that the 'voluntary' element becomes an excuse for changing full time jobs into part time jobs, e.g. at KP Foods in the UK full time (40 hours a week) jobs were converted into predominantly part time (25 hours a week jobs). The changeover was 'voluntary' - assisted by employees receiving two-thirds of the government grant under the job-splitting scheme - and, further aided by 15-20 per cent labour

turnover rates, was swiftly achieved.(1) The question of choice here for the existing full timers and for those who might seek employment at KP Foods in the future is debateable.

2 that employment contracts vary so much across the workforce that it becomes difficult to distinguish between what has been voluntarily agreed and what has become the enforced norm among groups of workers or in certain parts of the organization. Wide differentiation could then affect movement between jobs and between sections of the workforce, promotion prospects, pensions, equal treatment, etc. The question of a form of occupational apartheid based on hours of work is then raised.

3 that people become 'trapped' in the number of hours or the type of working patterns which they might happen to have chosen at some moment in time. Moving down in hours, for example when parental status is initially acquired, might not guarantee an ability to increase hours at a later date.

4 that over-emphasis on the voluntary approach breeds laissez-faire attitudes in regard to hours and remuneration. Choice in reducing hours can become an excuse for allowing excessive hours to be worked e.g. piecework systems in the clothing and 'fancy goods' industries, assisted by 'homeworking', offers 'choice' of hours; but low rates of pay usually mean long hours.

None of these dangers are totally insurmountable and progressive V-time initiatives might occur without such drawbacks. However, the desire to preach the gospel of choice has to be tempered by a practical appreciation of the problems involved. Total freedom of choice may well inhibit the freedom of others and - taken to a conclusion of unregulated 'hire and fire', work as and when you want to, type of system - might mean little choice at all. Choice has to be tempered by notions of 'fairness' and 'equal treatment', which is where collective bargaining ought to come in.

Future trends and directions - some possibilities

For the individual as well as for the negotiator and industrial relations specialist, the key question is - as Lenin put it - what is to be done? Does the market hold sway and a thousand flowers bloom - a number of which might turn out to be injurious to health - or should regulations and state intervention dominate? Different countries have adopted different mixes - few going totally one way or the other. When state intervention is generally limited to setting retirement ages and little else, such as in the United Kingdom (the recent lifting of regulations governing female nightshift workers removed one of the last statutory controls over hours), it would be foolish to expect a plethora of statutes governing overtime and working hours to emerge from any major political party. Thus, it can be safely assumed that future working time reductions will continue to be the province of voluntary decisions or negotiated agreements (or a combination of the two).

Despite considerable publicity since the European Trade Union Congress (ETUC) launched its drive for the 35-hour week in the late 1970s, progress on the shorter working week has been slow and appears to be slowing further. The numbers achieving hours reductions have declined throughout the 1980s. What this effectively means is that for full time male manual workers, the 39-hour week has become the norm - some 82 per cent of all male manual workers are now on a 39-hour week and a further 10 per cent on a 40-hour week - but progress beyond the 39-hour week has been isolated to a small number of well-publicized cases.(2) A one hour a week reduction in a period when unemployment has trebled in the United Kingdom seems scant reward for a decade of trade union endeavour.

Does this poor return make the shorter working week strategy redundant? Despite being critical of it, the answer would have to be a qualified no. Had the engineering unions (under the CSEU - Confederation of Shipbuilding and Engineering Unions) achieved an agreement on the 37½ hour week in this year's negotiations (an agreement blocked by the <u>union</u> side for whom a majority felt unhappy about the flexibility enabling proposals which the employers wanted in exchange for the 37½ hour week), it is quite likely that there would have been a major knock-on effect as the agreement would have directly covered some 800,000 workers. A similar knock-on effect was experienced following the last engineering union deal on the 39-hour week in 1979 (the only real major breakthrough in shorter weekly hours for the past decade). Equally, it is noticeable that the German metalworkers historic agreement on the 38½-hour week has had repercussions throughout German industry - the latest being the German steelworkers attainment of the 36-hour week. The strategy could produce dividends. However, where qualification is required concerns the emphasis and effort put into the campaign. Shorter weekly hours are not the <u>only</u> means of reducing working time - they are probably not even the best means (particularly where overtime goes unchecked). Promotion of other possibilities could produce better results (they would need to achieve very little not to) and, what is more important, might well arouse more public and employee support than that engendered by going home an hour earlier on Friday!(3) Certainly the survey evidence in this report would suggest a wider range of options.

As far as flexibility is concerned, the evidence (as stated) may be contradictory but the future direction ought to be clear. One of the most critical studies of the 'flexibility' thesis argued that it was not certain that the growth of part time, temporary work and self-employment was as a consequence of changes in the employment strategies of employers (other reasons suggested were structural shifts in employment patterns and recruitment difficulties).(4) Nevertheless, even were this true, there can be little doubt that these developments and greater personal flexibility will play an important part in employers' strategies of the future. The extent of flexibility may be limited at present, but the toughness of the Engineering Employers' Federation in demanding flexibility working provisions in return for the 37½ hour week ought to be some indication of employers' thinking. A cursory look at what is being attempted in the employer pacesetting organizations such as Ford and General Motors would serve to underline the importance of flexibility as a strategy, were it necessary to do so.

The drive for flexibility, particularly in the area of 'functional flexibility' (e.g. multi-skilling, simplified grading systems and greater job mobility/skill transfer), provides clear opportunities for renegotiated terms and conditions. For advocates of reduced hours there is a danger that such measures will be 'bought out' financially rather than through less working time. An examination of means of shortening the working year and the working life might prove more profitable and more attractive to employees, than an attempt to wring a further hour off the week out of employers.

For too long negotiators have been ignoring deep-seated underlying trends in the labour market and butting their heads against the brick wall of shorter weekly hours. It is about time they began to go with the flow. Studies show that the vast majority of part time workers and (perhaps surprisingly) about one-third of temporary workers elect and prefer to work under those arrangements. Neither are much concerned with reducing working hours. They are, however, very concerned about their contractual rights and entitlements - what may be termed a 'time contract'. Equally, full time workers seldom wish to lose income as a consequence of greater leisure time: means to improve the efficiency of what is done during those working hours would probably be welcomed in return for some tangible gain. Employees have difficulty in perceiving an hour off the working week as a tangible gain. An extra week's holiday a year, a four-day week or earlier retirement all have stronger appeals - particularly for 'middle-aged' and 'older' workers. Time contracts which emphasized <u>annual working time</u> would facilitate initiatives and innovations in all these areas.

Traditional Monday to Friday, 9 to 5 hours are a thing of the past. Some 25 per cent of the labour force work part time and 45 per cent of the working population work at weekends (though not necessarily regularly). Shiftwork is expanding and working patterns are being geared to technological and customer requirements rather than being based on notions of the traditional work week. The potential for greater employee choice over their working hours clearly exists. Too much emphasis on individual arrangements has pitfalls, a number of which have been mentioned, but employees' preferences should be listened to a lot more than they have been in the past. Employees, where given the option, have consistently voted for systems which optimize leisure blocks - even where this has meant 9, 10 and 12-hour shifts - and would appear to perceive working time in annual rather than weekly terms. A blending of employee preference with collective safeguards under a range of annual time contracts would seem the way forward best suited to the requirements of the individual and of the business. Where nothing is offered for nothing, a broader annual perspective on working time would appear to hold out the prospect of mutual benefits to employee and employer alike.

Notes

1. For a summary of the changes at K.P. Foods see <u>Industrial Relations Review and Report</u> - 'Greater productivity through flexibility', IRRR 405, 1 December 1987 pp. 9-11.
2. See, for example, <u>Industrial Relations Review and Report</u> - Reductions in working time - running out of steam? (IRRR 407, 12 January 1988) pp.2-6.
3. Although international survey data is patchy, one West German study showed only 19 per cent preferring shorter hours per day to 25 per cent who wanted a compressed working week and 53 per cent who wanted longer holidays and a further German study, which included early retirement as an option, found 89 per cent preferring options other than a shorter working day. See R. Cuvillier - <u>The Reduction of Working Time</u> (ILO, Geneva 1984). Thus, unless the shorter working week means a 3 or 4 day week, which it seldom does, employees would not appear to hold it in particularly high regard.
4. See Anna Pollert - 'The 'flexible firm': a model in search of reality?' <u>Warwick Paper in Industrial Relations</u>, No. 19 (Industrial Relations Research Unit, Warwick University, Coventry, 1988).

Select bibliography

Armstrong, P. (1984), *Technical Change and Reductions in life hours of Work*, Technical Change Centre, London.
Blyton, P. (1985), *Changes in Working Time: An international Review*, Croom Helm, London.
Brewster, C. and Connock, S. (1985), *Industrial Relations: Cost Effective Strategies*, Hutchinson, London.
Clutterbuck, D. and Hill, R. (1981), *The Re-making of Work*, Grant McIntyre, London.
Curson, C. (ed.), (1986), *Flexible Patterns of Work*, Institute of Personnel Management, London.
Cuvillier, R. (1984), *The Reduction of Working Time*, International Labour Office, Geneva.
Evans, A. and Palmer, S. (1985), *Negotiating Shorter Working Hours*, Macmillan, London.
Fragniere, G. (ed.) (1984), *The Future of Work*, Van Gorcum, Netherlands.
Gorz, A. (1985), *Paths to Paradise*, Pluto, London.
Handy, C. (1984), *The Future of Work*, Blackwell, Oxford
Hart, R. A. (1984), *Shorter Working Time: A Dilemma for Collective Bargaining*, OECD, Paris.
Hart, R. A. (1987), *Working Time and Employment*, Allen and Unwin, London.
Rathkey, P. (1984), *Work and the Prisoners of Time*, Work and Society, Brighton.
Rathkey, P. (1985), *Work Sharing and the Reduction and Reorganization of Work at Firm Level*, EEC, Brussels.
White, M. (1980), *Shorter Working Time*, Policy Studies Institute, London.

Appendix I
Survey questionnaire

Working time questionnaire

Name _____

Address _____

_____

_____

Telephone no. _____

Occupation of head of household
_____

Title _____

Industry or business _____

_____

Qualifications _____

_____

_____

Age _____

16–21	1
22–24	2
25–34	3
35–44	4
45–49	5
50–54	6
55–59	7
60–64	8

Sex _____

Male	1
Female	2

Social class _____

AB	1
C1	2
C2	3
D	4

Working Status

Full time (28+ hours)   1
Part time (less than 28 hours)   2

Number of hours worked per week (before overtime)   _____

Accommodation

Private rented   1
Public rented (council)   2
Owner occupied - with mortgage   3
Owner occupied - w/o mortgage   4

Industry category

Manufacturing   1
Transport & construction   2
Retail & consumer   3
Services & professional   4
Agriculture & materials   5
Other   6

Status in household

Head of household   1
Spouse of head of household   2
Neither   3

Trade union membership

Yes   1
No   2

Number of adults in household (16+)

Shiftworking

Always   1
Sometimes   2
Never   3

Children in household

With children under 5   1
With children 5-10   2
With children 11-15   3
No children under 16   4

1a Which of the words listed below would you use to describe your job?

 b Which of the words do not apply to your job?

   Apply to job   a
   Don't apply to job   b

boring	_____	frustrating	_____
challenging	_____	stressful	_____
varied	_____	rewarding	_____
tedious	_____	enjoyable	_____
strenuous	_____	exciting	_____
demanding	_____	repetitive	_____
none of these	_____		

Which other words would you use to describe your job?
_____

2 Being absolutely honest with yourself, how satisfying do you find your job?   _____

   Very satisfying   1
   Quite satisfying   2
   Not particularly satisfying   3
   Not at all satisfying   4
   Don't know/not sure   5

3 And in general how interesting do you find your job?   _____

   Very interesting   1
   Fairly interesting   2
   Pretty boring   3
   Very boring   4
   Don't know/not sure   5

4 Which hours of the day do you generally <u>like the most</u>; the hours you spend at work, the hours when you're not at work or both equally?

                                           _____
   Hours at work   1
   Hours outside work   2
   Both equally   3
   Don't know   4

5 And how satisfied are you with the basic wage you receive for your job? By basic, we mean your standard wage before any payments for overtime.   _____

   More than satisfied   1
   Quite satisfied   2
   Neither satisfied nor dissatisfied   3
   Less than satisfied   4
   Very dissatisfied   5
   Don't know/not sure   6

6   How often, on average, would you say that you work at weekends - by that we mean work either Saturday, Sunday or both? _____

    Every weekend   1
    Most weekends   2
    Occasional weekends   3
    Never work weekends   4
    Don't know/not sure   5

7a Do you ever have the opportunity to work <u>paid</u> overtime? _____

    Yes   1 -   **ASK b**
    No   2 -   **SKIP TO Q.7d**
    Don't know   3

b   How often do you get the chance to work <u>paid</u> overtime? _____

    Every week   1
    Most weeks   2
    Occasional weeks   3

c   On average how many hours a week <u>paid</u> overtime do you work? _____

    None   1
    1-5   2
    6-10   3
    11-15   4
    16-20   5
    20+   6

d   **ASK ALL**
    And on average how many hours a week <u>unpaid</u> overtime do you work?

    _____

    None   1
    1-5   2
    6-10   3
    11-15   4
    16-20   5
    20+   6

8   If you could choose how many hours paid overtime you could work, how many hours a week <u>paid</u> overtime would you work? _____

    None   1
    1-5   2
    6-10   3
    11-15   4
    16-20   5
    20+   6

Read out:

Now I'd like to ask you a few questions about the length of your contractual <u>working week</u> - by that we mean the number of hours you have to work each week before you do any overtime.

9a Over the last two years have your contractual (normal) hours of work increased, stayed about the same or decreased? _____

    Increased   1
    Decreased   2 - **ASK b, c**
    Stayed same   3
    Don't know/not sure   4 - **SKIP TO Q.11**

  b By roughly how many hours a week has it increased/decreased? _____

        0-1   1
        2-3   2
        4-5   3
        6-10   4
        11-15   5
        16-20   6
        20+   7

  c And who decided that your hours should change? _____

        Self   1
        Trade Union   2
        Employer   3
        Other (Write in)   4
                                                             5

ASK Q.10 IF RESPONDENT WORKS FULL TIME, OTHERS SKIP TO Q.11.

10a Do you work full time from choice? _____

    Yes   1
    No   2
    Don't know   3

  b And do you expect, or would you like, to work part time at some point in the future? _____

      Yes   1
      No   2
      Don't know   3

NOW SKIP TO Q.12

ASK Q.11 IF WORK PART TIME, OTHERS SKIP TO *.

11a Do you work part time from choice?

    Yes   1
    No   2
    Don't know   3

  b And do you expect, or would you like to work full time in the future?

    Yes   1
    No   2
    Don't know   3

* **READ OUT TO ALL**

I'd now like to ask you some questions about ways in which people can vary the way they work.
  Some of the ways may not be possible for you, <u>but</u> we would still like you to think about how you would <u>like</u> to work.

ASK ALL

12 **Say:** Here are three ways in which the number of hours you work could be reduced.
    If each of these schemes had the same effect on your wages and <u>if you could choose</u> one of them, which one would it be?

    Shorter hours each week   1
    Working the same hours each week but with longer annual holidays   2
    Working the same hours each week throughout your working life but then retiring earlier   3
    None of these (happy as I am)   4
    Don't know/not sure   5

13a If you could decide how many hours you worked, and you would earn proportionately more for working more hours and proportionately less for working less hours, which of these options would you choose?

(IF RESPONDENT SEEMS UNSURE EXPLAIN: If for example you were working a 35 hour week, earning £4 per hour, then your basic wage would be £140 per week. If you chose to reduce this by five hours a week then you would earn 5 x £4 a week less, i.e. from £140 down to £120 a week basic wage. Similarly if you chose to work 5 hours a week more, then your wage would increase by 5 x £4 i.e. from £140 to £160 a week).

    Work more hours for proportionately more pay   1 - **ASK b,c**
    Work less hours for proportionately less pay   2 - **SKIP TO d**
    Working the same hours as you do now for the same pay   3
    Not applicable to my job   4 - **SKIP TO Q.14**
    Don't know/not sure   5

b How many extra hours a week would you like to work? _____

```
1                                                              1
2                                                              2
3                                                              3
4-5                                                            4
6-10                                                           5
11-15                                                          6
16-20                                                          7
20+                                                            8
```

c Which, if any, of these prevents you from working more hours? _____

```
Hours fixed by contract                                        1
No/few overtime opportunities                                  2
Overtime is not paid                                           3
Other (WRITE IN)                                               4
Don't know/not sure/none of these                              5
```

SKIP TO Q.14.

ASK Q.13d IF YOU WANT TO WORK LESS HOURS AT Q.13a, OTHERS SKIP TO Q.14.

13d How many less hours a week would you like to work? _____

```
1                                                              1
2                                                              2
3                                                              3
4-5                                                            4
6-10                                                           5
11-15                                                          6
16-20                                                          7
20+                                                            8
```

e Which, if any, of these prevents you from working less hours? _____

```
Hours fixed by contract                                                     1
Need to work as many hours as I do because I need the money                 2
Need to work as many hours as I do to get the job done                      3
Other (WRITE IN)                                                            4
Don't know/not sure                                                         5
```

14 If you had a choice between working the same number of hours that you do now for more money, or working less hours than you do now but for the same wages as you get at the moment, which would you choose? _____

```
Higher wages and same hours                                    1
Same wages and less hours                                      2
Depends how much more/less                                     3
Don't know/not sure                                            4
```

15 **SAY:** If in the future you were given the choice of working less hours for the same pay which of the following six alternatives for reducing your hours would you prefer? _____

And which would be of least interest to you? _____

	Prefer	Least Interest
5 day working week with less working hours per day	1	1
4 day working week (with a slightly longer working day)	2	2
Same hours and days per week as you do now but with longer holidays	3	3
A longer period of education or training before beginning work	4	4
Sabbaticals (by that we mean paid time off one year for further study or doing something different before going back to work)	5	5
Earlier retirement	6	6
Don't know/not sure	7	7

16 I'd now like you to imagine that you work a 36-hour week. If your wages and benefits were unaffected which of the following working weeks would you prefer? _____

Five day week with a shorter working day,
e.g. 7 hours 12 minutes a day   1
Five day week with a shorter fifth day,
e.g. 4 days of 8 hours per day with a short 4-hour Friday   2
Longer hours per day but fewer days per week,
e.g. four day week with a 9-hour day
    3
Longer hours per day but fewer days per week,
e.g. three day week with a 12-hour day
    4
Don't know/not sure   5

17 Thinking now <u>just of your own job</u>, which of these options would you prefer: to work fewer days each week, but longer hours each day, or to work the same days and hours as you do at present? _____

Fewer days, but longer hours   1
Same days and hours as present   2
Don't know/not sure   3

18 You may have heard of a system called flexi-time. This is a system which allows you to work selected hours around a compulsory band of hours. For example, a person could work anytime between 7.00 a.m. to 6.00 p.m. with the period 10.00 a.m. to 4.00 p.m. being compulsory. Overall you will still have to work the same number of hours, but this system allows people a choice of which hours they want to work. You can also 'save up' hours by working more hours for some weeks and then using these hours for additional holidays.

a Do you have a flexi-time system in your present occupation? _____

    Yes   1 - CLOSE
    No   2
    Don't know   3 - ASK b

b If it were possible in your job, would you like to work a flexi-time system? _____

    Yes   1
    No   2
    Don't know   3
    Not applicable to my job   4

19a Using the table below, can you please indicate the range into which your average 'take home' income falls? _____

b And into which range does the average income of your <u>household</u> fall? _____

	Monthly	Weekly	
A	Up to £340	Less than £85	V
B	£ 341 - £ 480	£ 85 - £120	X
C	£ 481 - £ 640	£121 - £160	0
D	£ 641 - £ 880	£161 - £220	1
E	£ 881 - £1120	£221 - £280	2
F	£1121 - £1400	£281 - £350	3
G	£1401 - £1800	£351 - £450	4
H	£1801 - £2400	£451 - £600	5
I	£2,400 +	£600 +	6

Appendix II
Survey classification

Table 11.1

	Total	Age					Class				Age/Class				Sex/Class			
		16-24	25-34	35-44	45-54	55-64	AB	C1	C2	D	16-34 C1	35-64 C1	16-34 C2D	35-64 C2D	Male C1	Female C1	Male C2D	Female C2D
Total	523	97	142	135	110	39	94	138	198	93	74	64	129	162	77	61	171	120
Age:																		
16-21	57 / 11%	57 / 59%	0 / -	0 / -	0 / -	0 / -	7 / 7%	17 / 12%	21 / 11%	12 / 13%	17 / 23%	0 / -	33 / 26%	0 / -	9 / 12%	8 / 13%	20 / 12%	13 / 11%
22-24	40 / 8%	40 / 41%	0 / -	0 / -	0 / -	0 / -	4 / 4%	11 / 8%	16 / 8%	9 / 10%	11 / 15%	0 / -	25 / 19%	0 / -	6 / 8%	5 / 8%	11 / 6%	14 / 12%
25-34	142 / 27%	0 / -	142 / 100%	0 / -	0 / -	0 / -	25 / 27%	46 / 33%	47 / 24%	24 / 26%	46 / 62%	0 / -	71 / 55%	0 / -	28 / 36%	18 / 30%	50 / 29%	21 / 18%
35-44	135 / 26%	0 / -	0 / -	135 / 100%	0 / -	0 / -	31 / 33%	33 / 24%	50 / 25%	21 / 23%	0 / -	33 / 52%	0 / -	71 / 44%	19 / 25%	14 / 23%	37 / 22%	34 / 28%
45-49	69 / 13%	0 / -	0 / -	0 / -	69 / 63%	0 / -	11 / 12%	16 / 12%	33 / 17%	9 / 10%	0 / -	16 / 25%	0 / -	42 / 26%	7 / 9%	9 / 15%	20 / 12%	22 / 18%
50-54	41 / 8%	0 / -	0 / -	0 / -	41 / 37%	0 / -	8 / 9%	6 / 4%	17 / 9%	10 / 11%	0 / -	6 / 9%	0 / -	27 / 17%	3 / 4%	3 / 5%	20 / 12%	7 / 6%
55-59	31 / 8%	0 / -	0 / -	0 / -	0 / -	31 / 79%	6 / 6%	8 / 6%	12 / 9%	5 / 5%	0 / -	8 / 13%	0 / -	17 / 10%	4 / 5%	4 / 7%	9 / 5%	0 / -
60-64	8 / 2%	0 / -	0 / -	0 / -	0 / -	8 / 21%	2 / 2%	1 / 1%	2 / 1%	3 / 3%	0 / -	1 / 2%	0 / -	5 / 3%	1 / 1%	0 / -	4 / 2%	1 / 1%
Sex:																		
Male	308 / 59%	52 / 54%	95 / 67%	73 / 54%	63 / 57%	25 / 64%	60 / 64%	77 / 56%	118 / 60%	53 / 57%	43 / 58%	34 / 53%	81 / 63%	90 / 56%	77 / 100%	0 / -	171 / 100%	0 / -
Female	215 / 41%	45 / 46%	47 / 33%	62 / 46%	47 / 43%	14 / 36%	34 / 36%	61 / 44%	80 / 40%	40 / 43%	31 / 42%	30 / 47%	48 / 37%	72 / 44%	0 / -	61 / 100%	0 / -	120 / 100%

Table 11.2

	Total	Age					Class				Age/Class				Sex/Class			
		16-24	25-34	35-44	45-54	55-64	AB	C1	C2	D	16-34 C1	35-64 C1	16-34 C2D	35-64 C2D	Male C1	Female C1	Male C2D	Female C2D
Total	523	97	142	135	110	39	94	138	198	93	74	64	129	162	77	61	171	120
S.E.G.																		
AB	94 18%	11 11%	25 18%	31 23%	19 17%	8 21%	94 100%	0 -	0 -	0 -	0 -	0 -	0 -	0 -	0 -	0 -	0 -	0 -
C1	138	28	46	33	22	9	0	138	0	0	74	64	0	0	77	61	0	0
0																		
C2	198 38%	37 38%	47 33%	50 37%	50 45%	14 36%	-	100%	198 100%	-	100%	100%	84 65%	114 70%	100%	100%	118 69%	80 67%
D	93 18%	21 22%	24 17%	21 16%	19 17%	8 21%	0 -	0 -	0 -	93 100%	0 -	0 -	45 35%	48 30%	0 -	0 -	53 31%	40 33%

Working status

	Total	16-24	25-34	35-44	45-54	55-64	AB	C1	C2	D	16-34 C1	35-64 C1	16-34 C2D	35-64 C2D	Male C1	Female C1	Male C2D	Female C2D
Full time (28+ hours)	414 79%	91 94%	115 81%	99 73%	81 74%	28 72%	79 84%	114 83%	150 76%	71 76%	62 84%	52 81%	110 85%	111 69%	75 97%	39 64%	167 98%	54 45%
Part time (less than 28 hours)	109 21%	6 6%	27 19%	36 27%	29 26%	11 28%	15 16%	24 17%	48 24%	22 24%	12 16%	12 19%	19 15%	51 31%	2 3%	22 36%	4 2%	66 55%

Table 11.3

	Total	Age					Class				Age/Class				Sex/Class			
		16-24	25-34	35-44	45-54	55-64	AB	C1	C2	D	16-34 C1	35-64 C1	16-34 C2D	35-64 C2D	Male C1	Female C1	Male C2D	Female C2D
Total	523	97	142	135	110	39	94	138	198	93	74	64	129	162	77	61	171	120
Status in household:																		
Head of household	301 58%	25 26%	93 65%	85 63%	70 64%	28 72%	61 65%	81 59%	104 53%	55 59%	38 51%	43 67%	62 48%	97 60%	64 83%	17 28%	143 84%	16 13%
Spouse of head of household	144 28%	11 11%	37 26%	47 35%	38 35%	11 28%	21 22%	35 25%	66 33%	22 24%	14 19%	21 33%	26 20%	62 38%	1 1%	34 56%	0 -	88 73%
Neither	77 15%	61 63%	12 8%	3 2%	1 1%	0 -	11 12%	22 16%	28 14%	16 17%	22 30%	0 -	41 32%	3 2%	12 16%	10 16%	28 16%	16 13%
Children in household:																		
With children under 5	83 16%	9 9%	48 34%	22 16%	4 4%	0 -	15 16%	26 19%	26 13%	16 17%	19 26%	7 11%	27 21%	15 9%	19 25%	7 11%	36 21%	6 5%
With chidren 5-10	119 23%	2 2%	48 34%	52 39%	16 15%	1 3%	20 21%	33 24%	47 24%	19 20%	20 27%	13 20%	24 19%	42 26%	18 23%	15 25%	37 22%	29 24%
With chidren 11-15	131 25%	15 15%	19 13%	65 48%	28 25%	4 10%	24 26%	28 20%	55 28%	24 26%	8 11%	20 31%	23 18%	56 35%	17 22%	11 18%	41 24%	38 32%
No children under 16	272 52%	73 75%	58 41%	32 24%	74 67%	35 90%	48 51%	74 54%	101 51%	49 53%	39 53%	35 55%	72 56%	78 48%	37 48%	37 61%	84 49%	66 55%

Table 11.4

	Total	------Age------						------Class------					------Age/Class------					------Sex/Class------			
		16-24	25-34	35-44	45-54	55-64		AB	C1	C2	D	16-34 C1	16-34 C2D	35-64 C1	35-64 C2D	Male C1	Male C2D	Female C1	Female C2D
Total	523	97	142	135	110	39		94	138	198	93	74	129	64	162	77	171	61	120
Industry category:																				
Manufacturing	90 17%	15 15%	27 19%	20 15%	21 19%	7 18%		9 10%	21 15%	40 20%	20 22%	12 16%	28 22%	9 14%	32 20%	15 19%	45 26%	6 10%	15 13%
Transport and construction	53 10%	9 9%	19 13%	15 11%	7 6%	3 8%		5 5%	3 2%	33 17%	12 13%	2 3%	23 18%	1 2%	22 14%	3 4%	42 25%	0 -	3 3%
Retail and consumer	72 14%	16 16%	20 14%	21 16%	11 10%	4 10%		8 9%	25 18%	25 13%	14 15%	12 16%	21 16%	13 20%	18 11%	11 14%	14 8%	14 23%	25 21%
Services and professional	193 37%	33 34%	49 35%	48 36%	45 41%	18 46%		50 53%	60 43%	58 29%	25 27%	31 42%	32 25%	29 45%	51 31%	32 42%	30 18%	28 46%	53 44%
Agriculture and materials	10 2%	7 7%	1 1%	0 -	1 1%	1 3%		1 1%	1 1%	6 3%	2 2%	1 1%	6 5%	0 -	2 1%	1 1%	4 2%	0 -	4 3%
Other	105 20%	17 18%	26 18%	31 23%	25 23%	6 15%		21 22%	28 20%	36 18%	20 22%	16 22%	19 15%	12 19%	37 23%	15 19%	36 21%	13 21%	20 17%
Trade union member																				
Yes	206 39%	21 22%	63 44%	55 41%	49 45%	18 46%		36 38%	48 35%	86 43%	36 39%	23 31%	45 35%	25 39%	77 48%	31 40%	85 50%	17 28%	37 31%
No	317 61%	76 78%	79 56%	80 59%	61 55%	21 54%		58 62%	90 65%	112 57%	57 61%	51 69%	84 65%	39 61%	85 52%	46 60%	86 50%	44 72%	83 69%

Table 11.5

	Total	Age					Class				Age/Class				Sex/Class			
		16-24	25-34	35-44	45-54	55-64	AB	C1	C2	D	16-34 C1	35-64 C1	16-34 C2D	35-64 C2D	Male C1	Female C1	Male C2D	Female C2D
Total	523	97	142	135	110	39	94	138	198	93	74	64	129	162	77	61	171	120
Shift working																		
Always	81	12	24	14	26	5	8	16	37	20	9	7	23	34	13	3	42	15
	15%	12%	17%	10%	24%	13%	9%	12%	19%	22%	12%	11%	18%	21%	17%	5%	25%	13%
Sometimes	29	4	12	7	4	2	7	6	13	3	4	2	9	7	3	3	12	4
	6%	4%	8%	5%	4%	5%	7%	4%	7%	3%	5%	3%	7%	4%	4%	5%	7%	3%
Never	413	81	106	114	80	32	79	116	148	70	61	55	97	121	61	55	117	101
	79%	84%	75%	84%	73%	82%	84%	84%	75%	75%	82%	86%	75%	75%	79%	90%	68%	84%

Table 11.6

	Total	Age						Class				Age/Class					Sex/Class				
		16-24	25-34	35-44	45-54	55-64		AB	C1	C2	D	16-34 C1	35-64 C1	16-34 C2D	35-64 C2D		Male C1	Female C1	Male C2D	Female C2D
Total	523	97	142	135	110	39		94	138	198	93	74	64	129	162		77	61	171	120
Number of hours worked per week (before overtime)																					
Under 3	1 *	0	0	0	1 1%	0		1 1%	0	0	0		0	0	0	0		0	0	0	0
4-6 hrs	3 1%	0	0	1 1%	2 2%	0		1 1%	0	1 1%	1		0	0	0	1 1%		0	0	1 1%	1 2%
7-10 hrs	14 3%	0	3 2%	9 7%	2 2%	0		3 3%	2 1%	6 3%	3 3%		1 1%	1 2%	1 1%	8 5%		0	2 3%	0	9 8%
11-14 hrs	13 3%	0	4 3%	5 4%	3 3%	1 3%		1 1%	4 3%	5 3%	3 3%		1 1%	2 3%	2 2%	6 4%		0	4 7%	1 1%	7 6%
15-18 hrs	13 2%	1 1%	5 3%	2 1%	3 3%	3 8%		1 1%	3 3%	6 3%	3 3%		2 3%	2 3%	4 3%	5 3%		2 3%	2 3%	1 1%	9 8%
19-22 hrs	44 8%	4 4%	10 7%	14 10%	13 12%	3 8%		4 4%	9 7%	22 11%	9 10%		4 5%	5 8%	9 7%	22 14%		0	9 15%	4 2%	27 23%
23-26 hrs	10 2%	0	3 2%	3 2%	3 3%	1		2 2%	3 2%	3 2%	2 2%		2 3%	1 2%	1 1%	4 2%		0	3 5%	0	5 4%
27-30 hrs	15 3%	0	5 4%	6 4%	4 4%	0		6 6%	4 3%	4 2%	1 1%		2 3%	2 3%	3 2%	2 1%		1 1%	3 5%	0	5 4%
31-34 hrs	6 1%	1 1%	2 1%	2 1%	1 1%	0		1 1%	3 2%	1 1%	1 1%		2 3%	1 2%	1 1%	1 1%		2 3%	1 2%	0	2 2%
35-38 hrs	138 26%	33 34%	31 22%	36 27%	30 27%	8 21%		34 36%	39 28%	50 25%	15 16%		21 28%	18 28%	27 21%	38 23%		23 30%	16 26%	37 22%	28 23%
39-42 hrs	166 32%	46 47%	49 35%	32 24%	25 23%	14 36%		20 21%	45 33%	66 33%	35 38%		25 34%	20 31%	60 47%	41 25%		32 42%	13 21%	85 50%	16 13%
43-46 hrs	16 3%	3 3%	3 2%	4 3%	5 5%	1 3%		1 1%	2 1%	8 4%	5 5%		1 1%	1 2%	5 4%	8 5%		2 3%	0	12 7%	1 1%
47-50 hrs	17 3%	2 2%	6 4%	3 2%	5 5%	1		3 3%	6 4%	3 2%	5 5%		3 4%	3 5%	3 3%	4 2%		4 5%	2 3%	8 5%	0
51+ hrs	13 2%	1 1%	4 3%	6 4%	1 1%	1 3%		1 1%	4 3%	2 1%	6 6%		1 1%	5 8%	3 2%	5 3%		4 5%	0	8 5%	0
Dk/na	54 10%	6 6%	17 12%	12 9%	13 12%	6 15%		16 17%	13 9%	21 11%	4 4%		8 11%	5 8%	9 7%	16 10%		7 9%	6 10%	16 9%	9 8%
Mean	34.72	38.05	35.44	32.95	33.01	34.48		34.41	35.80	33.66	35.62		35.83	35.76	36.66	32.38		40.04	30.40	40.28	25.97

Table 11.7

	Total	Children in house		Head of household		Individual Wage (per month)				Household wage (per month)			
		0-4	5-15	Yes	No	Up to £480	£481-£880	£881-£1400	£1401+	Up to £480	£481-£880	£881-£1400	£1401+
Total	523	83	204	301	221	178	135	95	39	33	112	125	101
Age:													
16-21	57	6	14	9	48	38	13	1	1	5	8	7	5
	11%	7%	7%	3%	22%	21%	10%	1%	3%	15%	7%	6%	5%
22-24	40	3	3	16	24	17	15	4	1	3	9	7	6
	8%	4%	1%	5%	11%	10%	11%	4%	3%	9%	8%	6%	6%
25-34	142	48	57	93	49	38	42	33	11	5	42	42	27
	27%	58%	28%	31%	22%	21%	31%	35%	28%	15%	38%	34%	27%
35-44	135	22	93	85	50	41	27	36	12	10	23	35	36
	26%	27%	46%	28%	23%	23%	20%	38%	31%	30%	21%	28%	36%
45-49	69	3	25	39	29	29	17	10	3	8	16	17	11
	13%	4%	12%	13%	13%	16%	13%	11%	8%	24%	14%	14%	11%
50-54	41	1	8	31	10	7	12	6	4	0	9	8	8
	8%	1%	4%	10%	5%	4%	9%	6%	10%	-	8%	6%	8%
55-59	31	0	3	21	10	7	8	4	5	2	4	7	6
	6%	-	1%	7%	5%	4%	6%	4%	13%	6%	4%	6%	6%
60-64	8	0	1	7	1	1	1	1	2	0	1	2	2
	2%	-	*	2%	*	1%	1%	1%	5%	-	1%	2%	2%
Sex:													
Male	308	67	116	261	47	47	99	81	36	11	68	79	77
	59%	81%	57%	87%	21%	26%	73%	85%	92%	33%	61%	63%	76%
Female	215	16	88	40	174	131	36	14	3	22	44	46	24
	41%	19%	43%	13%	79%	74%	27%	15%	8%	67%	39%	37%	24%

Table 11.8

	Total	Children in house		Head of household		Individual Wage (per month)				Household wage (per month)			
		0-4	5-15	Yes	No	Up to £480	£481-£880	£881-£1400	£1401+	Up to £480	£481-£880	£881-£1400	£1401+
Total	523	83	204	301	221	178	135	95	39	33	112	125	101
Shift working													
Always	81	18	29	53	28	21	32	14	6	6	20	24	19
	15%	22%	14%	18%	13%	12%	24%	15%	15%	18%	18%	19%	19%
Sometimes	29	5	10	20	9	11	5	7	1	2	7	5	6
	6%	6%	5%	7%	4%	6%	4%	7%	3%	6%	6%	4%	6%
Never	413	60	165	228	184	146	98	74	32	25	85	96	76
	79%	72%	81%	76%	83%	82%	73%	78%	82%	76%	76%	77%	75%

Table 11.9

	Total	Working		Environment					Industry				TU Member		Ever-unemployed	
		Full-time	Part-time	Office	Factory	Services/Shop	Outdoor	Manufacturing	Transport and const	Retail and consumer	Services and prof	Agricultural and mater	Yes	No	Yes	No
Total	523	414	109	146	81	151	41	90	53	72	193	10	206	317	203	320
Age																
16-21	57	53	4	16	11	21	2	10	6	11	16	2	8	49	29	28
	11%	13%	4%	11%	14%	14%	5%	11%	11%	15%	8%	20%	4%	15%	14%	9%
22-24	40	38	2	12	6	13	3	5	3	5	17	5	13	27	18	22
	8%	9%	2%	8%	7%	9%	7%	6%	6%	7%	9%	50%	6%	9%	9%	7%
25-34	142	115	27	43	25	32	16	27	19	20	49	1	63	79	59	83
	27%	28%	25%	29%	31%	21%	39%	30%	36%	28%	25%	10%	31%	25%	29%	26%
35-44	135	99	36	34	18	41	10	20	15	21	48	0	55	80	40	95
	26%	24%	33%	23%	22%	27%	24%	22%	28%	29%	25%		27%	25%	20%	30%
45-49	69	47	22	18	6	28	2	10	4	7	30	1	27	42	27	42
	13%	11%	20%	12%	7%	19%	5%	11%	8%	10%	16%	10%	13%	13%	13%	13%
50-54	41	34	7	11	10	8	4	11	3	4	15	0	22	19	18	23
	8%	8%	6%	8%	12%	5%	10%	12%	6%	6%	8%		11%	6%	9%	7%
55-59	31	21	10	11	3	7	2	6	2	3	16	1	13	18	11	20
	6%	5%	9%	8%	4%	5%	5%	7%	4%	4%	8%	10%	6%	6%	5%	6%
60-64	8	7	1	1	2	1	2	1	1	1	2	0	5	3	1	7
	2%	2%	1%	1%	2%	1%	5%	1%	2%	1%	1%		2%	1%	*	2%
Sex																
Male	308	301	7	81	64	62	41	68	49	27	100	6	143	165	135	173
	59%	73%	6%	55%	79%	41%	100%	76%	92%	38%	52%	60%	69%	52%	67%	54%
Female	215	113	102	65	17	89	0	22	4	45	93	4	63	152	68	147
	41%	27%	94%	45%	21%	59%		24%	8%	63%	48%	40%	31%	48%	33%	46%

Table 11.10

	Total	Working		Environment					Industry					T U Member		Ever unemployed	
		Full-time	Part-time	Office	Factory	Services/Shop	Outdoor	Manufacturing	Transport and const	Retail and consumer	Services and prof	Agricultural and mater	Yes	No	Yes	No
Total	523	414	109	146	81	151	41	90	53	72	193	10	206	317	203	320
S.E.G.																
AB	94	79	15	54	1	15	0	9	5	8	50	1	36	58	20	74
	18%	19%	14%	37%	1%	10%	-	10%	9%	11%	26%	10%	17%	18%	10%	23%
C1	138	114	24	56	9	32	3	21	3	25	60	1	48	90	53	85
	26%	28%	22%	38%	11%	21%	7%	23%	6%	35%	31%	10%	23%	28%	26%	27%
C2	198	150	48	31	48	66	24	40	33	25	58	6	86	112	83	115
	38%	36%	44%	21%	59%	44%	59%	44%	62%	35%	30%	60%	42%	35%	41%	36%
D	93	71	22	5	23	38	14	20	12	14	25	2	36	57	47	46
	18%	17%	20%	3%	28%	25%	34%	22%	23%	19%	13%	20%	17%	18%	23%	14%
Working status																
Full-time (28+ hours)	414	414	0	122	78	98	40	84	53	48	146	9	180	234	169	245
	79%	100%	-	84%	96%	65%	98%	93%	100%	67%	76%	90%	87%	74%	83%	77%
Part-time (less than 28 hours)	109	0	109	24	3	53	1	6	0	24	47	1	26	83	34	75
	21%	-	100%	16%	4%	35%	2%	7%	-	33%	24%	10%	13%	26%	17%	23%
Accommodation																
Private rented	26	23	3	8	4	7	2	2	2	5	5	2	4	22	11	15
	5%	6%	3%	5%	5%	5%	5%	2%	4%	7%	3%	20%	2%	7%	5%	5%
Public rented (council)	64	50	14	9	14	23	7	10	9	11	14	0	30	34	35	29
	12%	12%	13%	6%	17%	15%	17%	11%	17%	15%	7%	-	15%	11%	17%	9%
Owner occupied (with mortgage)	385	306	79	117	57	108	28	69	36	53	154	8	152	233	135	250
	74%	74%	72%	80%	70%	72%	68%	77%	68%	74%	80%	80%	74%	74%	67%	78%
Owner occupied (without mortgage)	45	32	13	11	6	12	4	8	6	3	19	0	18	27	20	25
	9%	8%	12%	8%	7%	8%	10%	9%	11%	4%	10%	-	9%	9%	10%	8%
Other	3	3	0	1	0	1	0	1	0	0	1	0	2	1	2	1
	1%	1%	-	1%	-	1%	-	1%	-	-	1%	-	1%	*	1%	*